HANK BRODT
HOLOCAUST MEMOIRS

A CANDLE AND A PROMISE

DEBORAH DONNELLY

ISBN 9789492371188 (ebook)

ISBN 9789492371218 (paperback)

ISBN 9789493056671 (hardback)

Publisher: Amsterdam Publishers

info@amsterdampublishers.com

Copyright text © Deborah Donnelly, 2016

Cover photo: Victoria Eichenlaub

Hank Brodt Holocaust Memoirs is part of the series Holocaust Survivor Memoirs World War II

Winner Outstanding Creator Awards 2022

"But is there hope? Is there hope in memory? There must be. Without hope memory would be morbid and sterile. Without memory, hope would be empty of meaning, and above all, empty of gratitude."

Eli Wiesel, 2002

CONTENTS

FOREWORD

To mimic a question asked in every Jewish home at every Passover Seder, "Why is this memoir different from every other memoir about the Holocaust?" The answer is complex and simple at the same time.

This memoir is not about being a victim, although there are many victims in the telling. This memoir is not about Nazi atrocities and the loss of millions of souls but rather about lessons learned for future generations. This memoir is not about survival but it has everything to do with survival. This memoir is not about a life lost but rather about a life regained, a life repurposed and a life reimagined. This memoir is not about the past but rather about the future. This memoir is not about death but rather about life. This memoir is not about yesterday but rather about tomorrow.

There have been all too many Holocausts throughout the tortured history of mankind. Those who have survived the horrors of a Holocaust bear forever the physical and psychological scars of families and friends subjugated to unspeakable horrors for no other reason than "they were who they were." The pain and memories of these experiences never go away.

Yet amidst all of the horrors and all of the unspeakable crimes, the will to survive transcends into a mission to learn, to teach and to change the future. The lessons learned evolve into avowals of self-assertion, into affirmations against bullying, and most of all, into a deep faith that humanity's innate goodness will triumph over evil in whatever shape it assumes.

This Holocaust memoir is about rebirth; it's about using the past, no matter how horrific and painful, as a springboard for making humanity better; it's about a broken silence.

–Dr. *Howard B. Schechter*, Former Principal, John A. Forrest School, Fair Lawn, New Jersey, Principal, P.S. 158, New York, New York, Literary Scholar and Historian

PREFACE

My father, Hank Brodt (born in 1925 as Henek Brodt in Boryslaw, Poland), did not defeat his captors by surviving. He defeated them by living. This is not a story of a man who survived, but a story of a man who lived.

Through the years my father remained silent, suffering quietly with the memories of what he had witnessed and experienced, along with an overpowering sense of helplessness. As a Holocaust survivor, what he had seen and lived through was almost unimaginable, including the dehumanization, demoralization, and deaths of his Jewish family and friends, which took place while the world as a whole seemed to have turned its back. For years, my father kept his story bottled up inside. On rare occasions and only with a trusted few, he would share pieces of information, tiny fragments of his own history.

Then one day, my father began to share his story. The tapestry that he kept so well hidden for so many years finally began to unfold. His voice shook as he began to tell of the horrors that were part of his life. With a voice of uncertainty yet determination, he broke his silence and shared his experiences. Now, his voice is my voice, telling a story of a life well lived despite the traumatic experiences of his youth.

In these memoirs, he recounts his life story. On numerous occasions he told me that I was too young to understand. Now as an adult and a mental health clinician, and expert in traumatic stress, I still fail to understand. With the help of his new rabbi, my father came to the realization that he was aging, that time was not standing still. With prodding he finally broke his silence and was willing to share the horrors that he was unable to shake off. Some people deny that the Holocaust ever happened. He wanted me to document the prejudice he encountered and the hate turned deadly in writing.

I will never forget the phone call when my father said: "I decided to let you write my book." I made plans to visit him in North Carolina to gather information. Over numerous visits and telephone conversations, I asked questions that I had never dared to ask before. He preferred that I would not use a tape recorder and that we just sit and have conversations. So with paper and pen in hand we talked.

Armed with sensitivity and my professional skillset of a 34-year career as mental health clinician with expertise in trauma, I carefully monitored the pace of our conversations while simultaneously watching my father's body language and tone of voice. I was mindful that I did not want this project to result in his becoming unduly stressed. Frequently we stopped so that I could refocus on the here and now. Previously my father had given me his tape from the Shoah project as well as audiotapes from past interviews. All of these media could not prepare me for what I was about to hear, as they were sanitized, barely touching the surface, compared to the present story. However, it served me well in terms of dates and places.

To us, family and close friends, my father is so much more than a Holocaust survivor. It is my hope that you will see that despite his early life experiences and the atrocities he suffered under the Nazis, my dad did more than live; he embraced life and he was able to smile, laugh and dance.

Hank Brodt on his 90th birthday, surrounded by family
(December 2015)

WITNESS AND SURVIVOR

"In Hamlet, Shakespeare's despondent young protagonist ponders the ultimate question: "To be or not to be." But there are other compelling questions some of us must ask. For example, the question I face every day is: to remember or to forget? When I was no more than a small child, I was not free to attend school, play with friends, or practice my faith. Instead, I was a prisoner, putting in 16 to 18 hours a day of back-breaking labor."

Those were my opening words the first time I addressed a group on my experiences during the Holocaust. This must have been in 1973. I was nervous, talking to this Jewish youth group. My youngest daughter, Deborah, belonged to United Synagogue Youth, and they had never had a survivor come and share the hell that was a part of his earlier life. I had always taken great care to protect my children from that part of me. I wanted my daughters to grow up believing that the world was safe, and look ahead to a positive future. I wanted them to grow up innocent, not knowing that one human being could be so cruel to another. I also wanted to protect myself from the past which was – and actually still is –

painful beyond words. One day my youngest daughter – she can't have been more than six years old – asked why she did not have two grandmas. What do you tell a young child?

I have made a commitment that my experiences will not be buried with me upon my demise. The nature of the burden has shifted. It is no longer my children and my own sanity that I need to protect as much as the truth of what happened, the reality of the suffering endured by so many, the unspeakable crime against humanity that was the Holocaust.

In 2007 during the Holocaust Remembrance services at Birkenau, the site of one of the concentration camps, Rabbi Fred Guttman arranged for me to light one of the six candles memorializing those who died. As I lit my candle, I said a silent prayer for those who died and could not speak for themselves. This extensive list included my mother, my sisters and their children, all victims of Hitler and his so-called Final Solution. I made a promise to all of them and to my brother, who I believed to have died fighting the Nazis, that I would always answer the call to talk.

I have now celebrated my 90th birthday, and am forced to admit that I am aging and that many of my friends who were also survivors have died. I feel obliged to speak for those who did not have the chance to speak for themselves. They were sadistically silenced for the crime of their faith or for not belonging to what they referred to as 'the master race'. So in essence, I have found the answer to the question that has haunted me for decades: to remember or to forget? I have to remember so that in sharing my story I know that I am doing all I can to ensure that no one forgets.

I dedicate *A Candle and a Promise* to the six million Jewish people who were murdered, as well as the countless other millions who perished under Hitler's regime. I also include all the survivors who locked away their memories for self-preservation and were unable to tell their stories. I know that for most of us, the post-war years were difficult and painful at best.

I humbly speak for all of you, so the world will never forget. I also dedicate this book to all in the military who put themselves at risk to stop the Nazis from murdering those that they did not see worthy of life, and prevent Hitler from coming to the United States.

On a personal level I dedicate my memoirs to my daughters, Evy and Deb, as this is very much a part of our family history. I thank Rabbi Guttman for helping me find my voice.

Despite all that happened I never lost my faith or belief in G-d. My relationship with G-d is personal. I am not sure whether I can forgive the Nazis for what they did. But I will certainly never forget.

As for those impossible questions, for some there are simply no answers. We are now more than seven decades removed and people still struggle to comprehend what happened, the full scale of the horrors of the Holocaust, the unimaginable evil, the stories and images that eventually emerged and stunned the world. Maybe it is not surprising, therefore, that there are still some who deny that the Holocaust ever happened. Even in the face of incontrovertible evidence, the magnitude of it is just too much for some to take in. But it did happen, it was real, and in the pages to follow, I will do what I could not do for so many years, which is share my own story. It has been buried in the depths of my memory, locked away to protect those I love.

As I look around and see that we did not learn the lessons of genocide and hatred, I understand that the world needs all the reminders of the past that we can generate. It is for that reason more than any other that I break my silence of sorrow and horror. I feel that it is important that children are taught that it is all right to be different, to have a different religion and race. We are all human beings.

So help me G-d, what I am about to say is the whole truth and nothing but the truth. I made a silent promise as the flame of the candle of remembrance flared up towards the heavens, solidifying my vow to speak for you.

Presentation at ForsythTech in Winston-Salem, NC (December 2015)

FAMILY AND EARLY YEARS

I don't have to try too hard when I close my eyes to see my mother's beautiful green eyes in her gaunt face. I can still hear her telling me to go outside and play with my friends. Even at the age of six – still six months shy of my seventh birthday – I helped my mother with chores around our two-room home in Boryslaw, the town in Poland where I was born.[1] It was the sort of small house one might expect of a very poor family, but my mother was fastidious in making sure it stayed clean.

There were a few pictures scattered around the house, photographs of my father, brother, sister and me. I was the youngest of three children. My brother, Simcha, was seven years my senior and my beautiful, sweet sister Faiga was eleven years older. My mother was a widow.

I don't remember my father, as he died when I was only eight months old. He had three other daughters from his first marriage: Frieda, Yetta and Doris. Sadly, I only met two of my half-sisters. For several years, I thought they were my aunts. It was not until I was older that Simcha explained their relationship to me.

Simcha was known as the scholar. He finished public school and went to university on some sort of scholarship. An excellent student without financial means, his studies were paid for by the Jewish Cultural Group of Boryslaw and Drohobycz.[2] After graduation, Simcha held a job in the alcohol division of the Polish government.

Faiga was quite simply a natural beauty. After completing public education, she studied to become a beautician. She was an apprentice in a kind of beauty salon. While she learned her trade, she needed to pay room and board in the beauty shop owner's home. It was a trying period for her. Not only was she working in the salon, she also had to cobble together the means to pay for this training and living expenses.

My mother did all that she could to support our family. Once Faiga had left home to pursue her dreams of becoming a beautician, living several kilometers away, our already meager income diminished. Simcha was also living out of the family home. The financial situation for the family, which had always been tenuous at best, was becoming more and more dire.

My mother was loving and very hard-working. It was not easy for a widow in those days to earn a wage. There was no life insurance payout when my father was tragically killed in an accident while on the job, leaving our family emotionally and financially devastated.

In an effort to put food on our table, my mother did everything she could. She worked several odd jobs, anything she could find that paid at least a little something. She cooked Shabbat dinner for wealthier families, baked for non-Jewish families during their holidays, took in ironing, and tended to the sick by providing mechanical leeching.[3]

Despite her medical know-how, my mother was not a healthy woman. She had a limp, always seemed tired and had poor vision. She underwent eye surgery, and though the surgery was considered to have been successful, it did more damage to her already diminished sight. Her health was a source of constant struggle, a battle she fought valiantly, though with each passing year she seemed to lose more ground.

Despite our financial difficulties, we lived in a conservative kosher home. We went to synagogue every Shabbat. We celebrated the holidays by attending services. While we could not afford to have elaborate meals as part of our holiday traditions, there were always wonderful smells coming from the kitchen; my mother was very creative. Saturday was a day of rest. We did not do any type of work on Shabbat. There was no writing or taking transportation. We remained steadfast in the practice of our faith.

Being kosher is not easy. Today it is not uncommon for an observant family to have a minimum of four sets of dishes: one set for dairy, one for meat, and two sets for Passover. Some kosher homes even have two sinks. We did not have the luxury of such a variety of dishes. We felt fortunate and content to own one set. The same plates were used for dairy, meat, and Passover.

We were proud of our religion and traditions. We were proud to be part of a strong Jewish community. The Cultural Center of Boryslaw and Drohobycz was an integral part of my family's life. Antisemitism existed and we could certainly perceive it very clearly, but nothing could prepare us for the hatred and crimes against humanity that would soon come.

When I lived in Boryslaw, the population of it and surrounding towns consisted of Polish and Ukrainian people. Neither the Polish nor the Ukrainians were ever friendly towards us Jews.

A MOTHER'S DIFFICULT DECISION

Even as a six-year-old, I noticed a profound change in my mother after Faiga and Simcha left home. I could not comprehend the change in mood in our home. When I tried to sleep at night, I heard my mother walking around the house crying. I did everything I could to please her, so I could not understand her tears. In addition to helping her around the house without being asked, I followed every direction she gave me. So why was she crying? What was wrong?

One day she told me to go and play. Off I went, with no reason to expect anything unusual. As I opened the door, I saw our rabbi and another well-dressed man standing outside. I gave him a polite greeting and my mother welcomed him into our home.

Outside were my best friends, Joseph, Juhuda and Abe. Joseph lived next door. At that time, my friends and I were looking forward to starting school in Boryslaw. I could hardly wait to learn to read, do math, and learn a trade so that I could help my mother.

As I approached my friends, Joseph passed me a ball that was maybe double the size of a tennis ball. We played something that resembled soccer, kicking the ball back and forth, laughing and just having fun. Then something caught my eye: Simcha and Faiga passed by, without acknowledging me. Now I thought that was strange, as Simcha would always join in the fun, and Faiga would stop and throw her arms around me, always happy to see me. For some odd reason, they seemed to be in a rush. We continued to play our version of soccer until I heard my mother call my name. Her voice was weak and hollow, and as I entered the house I could see that she had been crying. We all sat down to eat but Faiga looked strange, different than I had ever seen her. Her beautiful green eyes lacked the usual sparkle. It was unsettling to see her this way.

My mother had made one of my favorite foods. It was similar to what we call noodles, but much thicker and baked. Some butter, which had become scarce in our household, made this dish taste even better. Everyone was quiet as we ate, which added a somber note to our meal. There was a palpable tension that I could then not understand, though I understand it all too well now. What I did not know, could not have known or comprehended, was that my mother, our rabbi, and the other man, as well as my siblings, had been talking about me, without my being present. But what exactly had they been talking about?

After we finished our meal and cleaning up, my mother hugged me as if it were the last time. I suppose that in a way, it actually was. She told me that I would be going away to live in a Jewish home for children. She was sending me to an orphanage! I would be attending a public school in Drohobycz while living in the orphanage. Many Jewish families where one parent was deceased or in which a child had been orphaned used this 'social service'. Even some families that were simply too poor to care for their children sent them there. What choice did they have?

The orphanage was managed under the auspices of the Jewish Cultural Center. Even in the worst of circumstances, the Jewish population tried to take care of its own people. My poor mother could not stop crying. She was inconsolable, but she felt that there was just no other choice. She reassured me that she loved me and wanted me to be well cared for. I needed food, shelter, and schooling. My brother and sister each came to give me a hug, telling me how much they loved me. Faiga pleaded with me not to cry, since this was already so excruciatingly painful for our mama. Imagine any mother having to make this kind of decision. The Jewish Cultural Center was a social service but did not believe in keeping children in their family unit. I had no choice but to accept it. I would soon be leaving home, along with everything and everyone I knew and loved.

ORPHANAGE

I am afraid that I do not remember much about this period in my life. Being taken away from your family is a trauma that can easily distort the memory. When one takes into consideration my young age and the horrors yet to be experienced in the Holocaust, I suppose it will come as no surprise that many of the details of my life in the orphanage are either blurry or lost completely.

I do remember quite vividly being homesick and missing my mother. I felt utterly abandoned. The rules at the orphanage were very strict, and even the slightest infraction led to corporal punishment. We had daily chores and had to keep our sleeping area in immaculate condition. I slept in a large room where there were rows of beds. We had our meals in a large dining hall. Housed within the orphanage was a synagogue. This synagogue was an active part of the Jewish community, attended by members who also helped to support the orphanage. Every morning we would go into the sanctuary and recite our daily prayers. The Shabbat was no exception; most of Saturday was spent in devotion to God.

I finally got my wish and began to attend a public school, the Adam Mickiewicz School in Drohobycz. I loved to learn. It was in this school that I had my first experience of antisemitism. These days, there are frequent headlines about bullying in our schools. I can tell you that bullying is nothing new. It was certainly commonplace in Drohobycz in the 1930s. I was Jewish and lived in a residential setting, an orphanage. We were prime targets to be picked on by Jewish and non-Jewish children alike. Fighting back did not seem to be the answer. It certainly did nothing to dissuade the bullies. However, at times we were left with no choice.

Close to the Adam Mickiewicz School was a private Ukrainian school, seemingly for both a typical education as well as acquiring knowledge related to culture and religion. The pupils from there would taunt and physically assault one of the children from the orphanage on almost a daily basis. While we would fight amongst each other, we stood steadfast to defend our own. Often there were scenes that resembled the rumbles from the movie *West Side Story*. Protecting our brothers and sisters from physical and emotional abuse unfortunately resulted in earning us corporal punishment from our caregivers at the end of the day. I always believed that in families we protect our own. In essence we were family, brought together by our own unique circumstances. About the corporal punishment there was nothing much to be done but to learn to accept and endure it. I would always try to fight against bullying.

Fortunately, there were some better experiences that helped me during my tenure at both the orphanage and school. For example, my love of dogs goes back to one of my favorite teachers, Mr. Dumin. He owned a Doberman Pinscher named Viera. Upon his command, Viera would jump and remove Mr. Dumin's hat, placing it on the coat rack in the classroom. She listened to her master, followed every command, including 'sit', and we could pet her as long as we liked. Viera was an intelligent and gentle dog.

It was this positive experience with dogs that would prove invaluable in getting me through the SS commanding their dogs to attack prisoners. Many in the SS had German Shepherds and Doberman Pinschers at their command, trained to attack. These large dogs would maul helpless Jewish and non-Jewish people to their death. I stood by more times than I care to remember and saw it with my own young, unbelieving eyes. From the ghetto to the concentration camps, this appeared to be a favorite form of torture for those not part of the master race. Through my experience with Mr. Dumin, I learned that the dogs themselves were not evil. The only ones we had to fear were those trained to do the devil's bidding.

Visiting days in the orphanage were limited to one Saturday per month. My mother did not travel on Saturday due to Shabbat. Travel to Drohobycz was also expensive, which, given our impoverished circumstances, contributed to the lack of visits. Through all of my time in the orphanage, I remember only one visit from my mother. I had become sick with a very high fever. I was in and out of consciousness and thought I could hear my mother's footsteps. My mother, with her limp, had a very distinct gait with a unique sound that resonated in a room or hallway. I do not recall exactly what happened during this visit, but I do know that I returned to health, which was probably not a coincidence.

Other children had regular visits where they received many delicious goodies. When goodies were given, everyone shared with one another. I do have some fond memories of playing with the other children. I was athletic and enjoyed all games that were played with a ball.

Along with our chores in the orphanage, at times we were assigned tasks at the synagogue. One day a friend of mine and I were asked to clean it. It was understood that you did not snitch on a friend, an unwritten rule and a promise that I keep to this day. As we were cleaning the synagogue, we came across the cantor's bottle of vodka. We agreed that hard work deserved some type of compensation so we each took a small swig. We checked the bottle and didn't think the little we took would be noticed and so continued with our chores.

A few days later, when we were back doing work at the synagogue, we each took a slightly bigger sip. It occurred to us that there might be enough vodka missing now to be noticeable, which would result in potential disaster for both of us. So we added a bit of water, thinking that would be enough to conceal our little 'crime'. Each time we took a few more sips, enjoying the high and even more not being caught. We drank enough to get drunk, but were careful to cover our tracks by adding more water. On the fourth occasion our luck ran out. The cantor noticed that his beloved vodka did just not taste the same. Most likely, it was not providing the euphoria that he was used to enjoying.

There was no way around it. We were caught, as we were the only ones assigned chores at the synagogue. Since I was a bit more robust than my companion, I took full responsibility and saved at least one of us from the beating that ensued.

Much to my surprise, time was passing quickly. As I recall, I relished the few visits from Faiga during my stay in the orphanage, which lasted about six years, until the fall of 1939. I do remember that she came more often than Simcha, and that I was happy to see her.

I would be going home after my Bar Mitzvah, when I completed 7th grade. The Bar Mitzvah, for those who may not know, is a religious rite of passage in which a 13-year-old boy is transformed into a man. The Bar Mitzvahs at that time were only religious ceremonies. We did not have the elaborate parties that typically follow Bar Mitzvahs nowadays.

Group portrait of children and staff of the Jewish Orphanage in Drohobycz © United States Holocaust Memorial Museum, courtesy of Paul Leopold Lustig, 1921

RETURN HOME, 1939

I came home two weeks before the start of the war, when the Germans invaded Poland. However, home was no longer the same. We were all older now, which brought several life-changing events. Simcha had married his girlfriend, Andzia, and together they set up their own home.

Faiga was married to a fellow named Simcha Wald. Just as she had dreamed of, my sister had become a talented beautician and was working in Drohobycz. I was home and planning to contribute as a man should. I set out to find work and earn a wage to ensure that my mother would be well taken care of. She certainly needed it. She had become so terribly thin and frail, looking much, much older than her years. I was awfully worried about her. As always, I wanted to do anything I could to help her, but now this instinct was amplified a hundredfold. I felt helpless when I looked at her, but I was determined to do whatever I could to make her life better.

In a short time, our world would once again change. I remember looking at the houses near my own with their open spaces for a backyard. I missed the days when Joseph, Juhuda, Abe and I would play, so carefree, so oblivious to our futures.

In the fall of 1939, despite having signed the German-Polish Non-Aggression Pact in 1934, Germany marched into Poland. The Polish army, on horseback with soldiers bearing swords and rifles, was no match for the well-oiled German warmachine. Armed with tanks and with a superior air force, Germany swiftly defeated Poland.

Very soon afterwards, the Germans marched into my town. Though their stay was brief, they left an indelible mark on the Jewish population in the form of insults and humiliation. Russia matched Germany by taking over the Galicia region, the south-eastern part of Poland (which is currently part of Ukraine). Both my town and the Galicia region were now under Russian occupation.

The air was crisp and there was a faint smell of burning wood when we walked out of the synagogue at the conclusion of the High Holy Days. Could our prayers have been answered? Yes, the Germans were gone, but now the Russians had taken over. High above us, the loudspeakers were blaring Russian music. When the Russian music was not playing, the voice on the loudspeaker would tell us about the communist ways.

We had little time to get used to this new way of life before things changed again. My brother Simcha was drafted into the Red Army. He served on the frontlines during the war. Wherever Russia was fighting, that was where my brother went. Wherever the Russians ruled, people lost homes, farms, and businesses. That was the communist way. Regardless of how hard someone might have worked to build up a business, everything now belonged to the state. Without warning, people were being pushed out of their homes, while others shared their businesses that had been in the family for decades. We were poor and in an ironic sense I suppose this was lucky, as we did not have anything to give to the communist way of life. My mother and I were able to remain in our small home. But we could no longer pray in the synagogue, since all religions were now banned. Communism was the highest power of all. It was the new religion.

Life under communism served me well in one way. I trained as a lathe operator and could finally achieve my goal of getting a job. At long last, I would be able to support my mother!

Overall, life under the Russians presented its own set of difficulties. Most pressing was the shortage of food, especially sugar, flour and bread. Food in general was hard to come by, and before long the government began to ration it. Fuel was also in demand. Valuable resources became increasingly scarce. For example, it was almost impossible to find a doctor when you needed one. There were lines everywhere, stretching in all directions. For food, rationing cards, any available medical care. Sometimes it seemed that all people did was stand in lines. When supplies were not available for all of us, the black market was an option. We knew enough to avoid this at all costs, because the punishment could be severe.

Under the Russians, I got my first job, working on typewriters. As we adapted to the Russian language, the letters had to be changed. This was tedious work, and very labor intensive, as each key was carefully changed one at a time. For a young man of 13, this was miserably boring. I was full of energy and wanted to be doing more, though I did discover that I loved working with my hands.

Barely able to contain my happiness when I received my first paycheck, I proudly brought home my earnings and handed over the entire sum to my mother. I will never forget her tears of gratitude. It was perhaps the proudest moment of my life, or certainly one of my proudest moments. I was thrilled and gratified to have finally done it. Despite the tough times, we had some means of supporting ourselves.

MY CRIME

I worked long hours. We would work five-day rotations with one day off. I was young and still yearned for carefree days, but the responsibilities of work made those seem very remote. I did still manage to find time to play with my friends in the evenings. Under the darkening sky, we found some joy and some escape in the game of soccer. It was a way to run around and let the long days of hard work recede for a few precious minutes. After some playtime, it was time to eat and then off to bed for some badly needed rest.

One morning I committed a crime as far as the laws of Bolshevism were concerned. I know what you must be thinking. What crime could a 13-year-old boy with good values commit? I arrived late to work, although it cannot have been by more than ten to fifteen minutes. My boss actually filed charges against me, and I was called into a hearing before a magistrate. This proceeding was something similar to a court hearing.

Under Bolshevik law, there was an actual process in place in the criminal justice system for crimes that occurred in the workplace. As I stood in the small room, I noticed many other people. I couldn't help but wonder what they had done to be here. When my turn came, I walked up to the desk. A man I had seen at work told the magistrate that I had been late.

What could I say, even if I was given the chance? Before I had time to process what was happening, I was given my sentence: my paycheck would be reduced by ten per cent for several months! As I left the building, I felt depression coiling around me. My earnings were already meager, and now it would be even worse. Once again, I promised myself that I would take care of my mother regardless of this setback. My brother and sister were depending on me to take care of her. How were we going to get by with less money?

I was sure that my mother would be angry with me for being so careless with my time. I felt as if I had let her down and could hardly stand to face her after making such a catastrophic mistake. How would she react? To my surprise and great relief, she did not scold or reprimand me. Even with this significant cut in income, she managed to adjust our budget to buy what we needed. Of course, our food intake was much lower in those days. I could see that my mother was becoming increasingly weak. Yes, we were hungry, but our hunger then was nothing compared to what it would be.

RETURN OF THE NAZIS

In the days of the Nazis, whenever a 'non-aggression pact' was offered by Germany, it was sure to lead to a blitzkrieg. So, on June 22, 1941, the Nazis were back in Boryslaw. As before, they left blood and destruction in their wake. Many residents had bitter memories of Germany's few days in our area back in 1939.

Days after the victory against Russia, the first *Aktion*, a Nazi strategy to eliminate enemies, took place in Boryslaw. It targeted Polish intellectuals and members of the upper class. Unknown to us, Ukrainian leaders approached the Gestapo requesting that they be allowed to deal with the Jews. We did not know until well after the war that the Ukrainians and Poles who lived in the Galicia region blamed the Jews for supporting Bolshevism. The Germans gave the Ukrainians free reign to deal with us. The Ukrainians came from Boryslaw, Drohobycz and other nearby villages. They came in droves, with scythes and sickles in their hands, which they used to slaughter and maim people in the streets. The roads were literally stained red with blood.

My mother made the decision that neither of us would leave the house until this passed. We did all we could do, praying together that it would all end soon. During this period, we did not leave our house even to attend to our needs in the outhouse. It was too dangerous to go out for any reason at all. As we held our breath, we tried to comprehend this hatred against us from people we did not even know. What had we done? What had any of the Jewish people done to deserve this? We had no idea. We were confused, but mostly we were terrified.

Three days later the Nazis put a stop to this *Aktion* initiated and primarily carried out by Ukrainians. The Nazis including the SS ended it, killing any Jews left in sight. Then all Jews were ordered out of their homes by the Gestapo to 'clean up our mess' on the streets. That mess consisted mostly of the injured bodies of the victims: someone's mother, brother, father or friend. We picked up what remained of our loved ones and put them on pushcarts, and then prepared them for burial under the Jewish rites. They were buried in the Jewish cemetery of Boryslaw.

As in all other towns across Europe, a Jewish committee, or *Judenrat*, was formed. The Jewish committee in Boryslaw was headed by Michael Herz and other prominent leaders from our community. Their role was to serve as a liaison between the Gestapo assigned to our town and the Jewish community. The committee would supply the Nazis with names of all the Jewish people in town as well as provide workers, i.e. slave labor, for the German war effort.

New laws and edicts on how Jews were to be treated or rather mistreated came out on a regular basis. These edicts limited our ability to move around freely, own businesses and access services. Jewish businesses were handed over to others. Jews were not permitted to enter most stores to purchase even basic items. We were forbidden to walk on certain streets, to walk on the sidewalks, or to go into a cinema. If we passed a *Volksdeutsche* [person of

German ethnicity] we had to bow, remove our caps, and make way for them to pass. The buildings that were once our houses of worship were all burned to the ground.

All of those identified as Jews were given armbands to wear with an eight-point Star of David. In the middle of this yellow star was the word *Jude* or Jew. In Polish this armband was called *opaska*. We were now officially marked, in the literal sense. Failure to wear the *opaska* would result in being arrested or even death.

Jews were harassed daily. This harassment became our way of life. The orthodox Jews were especially picked on as they looked different, with their long beards and *payot*, Yiddish for side locks or side curls. As I walked, I watched a boy about my own age take a knife out of his pocket and chop off part of a religious man's beard as the police looked on and laughed. They ridiculed the man while he and his family stood helpless. I wish I could say that I only witnessed that one time. It is impossible to count the number of times I saw this type of harassment. If cutting one side of the payot was not bad enough, they seemed to purposefully slice into the person's skin.

I found myself becoming more and more enraged. There was no outlet to rid myself of the anger and hatred that were building inside me. There was nothing I could do but carry it around and feel it grow day by day. I watched my mother become weaker as the days wore on, and there was nothing I could do to stop it. That feeling of helplessness added to my anger.

As I walked through my town, orders were barked in German. Failure to comply resulted in being beaten or killed. Memorizing German words to avoid being clubbed, or worse killed, for not responding became very important. Fortunately, there was some similarity between German and Yiddish. I worked diligently to give these new German words meaning. I thought it might well mean the difference between life and death for me and my mother.

We did not know how it could get worse, but it did. I lost my job, our sole source of income. Our world was falling apart. By October 1941, things became even tougher. Two ghettos were formed in Boryslaw. There was no need for a fence. Most of us did not venture beyond our designated area. The Nazi guards and the Ukrainians, primarily the latter, gladly took on the job of beating any Jew who violated the rules or ventured beyond the ghetto.

Being poor did have some unexpected advantages in these miserable circumstances, and in a very strange way, we were actually lucky. Our house was in a poor section of town that was later designated the ghetto. As a result, we did not have to move and no one came to share our home. Unlike many others, we were not forced to endure such changes.

The *Judenrat*, which was responsible for providing jobs to the Jewish population, gave me the role of messenger. This allowed me to leave the ghetto, having the appropriate paperwork. Since some members of the Jewish community were not physically able to perform the jobs that were being assigned, it was not uncommon for others like myself to step up and work in their place.

I readily volunteered to work for other Jews who did not want to leave their homes or were unable to work for whatever reason. By assuming their identity, I earned a bit of money from the individual with the work duty. In addition, I was given food in exchange for my labor. The Jewish committee tried to feed as many people as possible. There was a community kitchen where people could come for some soup or a very simple meal. I would eat and in a metal container bring some food home for my mother who by this time hardly left her bed. I found that my earlier training at the orphanage came in handy. I was the equivalent to what is now referred to as street-smart. I had survival skills, was acutely aware of my surroundings and put up my own personal resistance to all that the Germans and Ukrainians were doing to the Jews. I was young and never thought of personal danger. I was invincible! I also kept true to my personal code of never being a snitch.

Unfortunately, not everyone lived according to that code. In all fairness, these circumstances have a way of bringing out the worst in people. The Jewish police were an example. Some would conspire with the Nazis and turn their best friends in. Most of the Jewish police were unaware at the time that they would eventually meet the same fate as the Jewish population at large. The Nazis would make no exception for them. The commander of the Jewish police must have predicted that he and his family would not be spared and tried to go into hiding. This man had a dog that he loved. This dog happened to be a barker. The commander killed his dog so it would not betray their hiding place when the time came.

When I finished work I was invited to play soccer. Many times, due to my work, I was outside of the ghetto. We would break into teams and play our hearts out. One day it was hot and I, along with others, took off my shirt and my *opaska*. When the game was over I put them back on. One young man said to me, "Why are you putting that on, look at you, you don't look Jewish, stay on this side, no one will know." The point was I would know and I had someone depending on me who could not venture out into the forbidden zone, she was too sick. Those times we met up to play soccer there was no segregation imposed by the Nazis, just a group of Polish teens having fun. I was always chosen first. I had a reputation as a very good soccer player.

LIFE GETS WORSE

As the days ran together, one interminably miserable day after the next, it became obvious that people were beginning to disappear. No one had answers, or those who might have had answers chose not to share them. I heard stories of the wealthier among us being able to bribe the guards consisting of Poles, Ukrainians, and Germans. None of the guards were above taking a bribe. Bribes included family heirlooms, jewelry, and money. Soon after the Germans came back, every Jewish family had to turn in their furs, silver and gold jewelry, whether it was a pair of Shabbat candle holders, picture frames, or a wedding ring. It did not make any difference. If it was silver or gold, we had to turn it in. For many, they were turning in something more valuable than gold or silver. These were pieces of their family history, heirlooms that should have gone to the next generation and beyond. It was amazing that there was anything left later on to use as a bribe.

Our general health also declined dramatically. Typhus and dysentery were common in the ghetto. We were not allowed medication. Even those who had the money could not buy it. The only way to obtain medicine was on the black market. There were still some Jewish physicians, but they were in the same circumstances as the rest of us.

My mother and I did not really feel any poorer than we ever had. We had so little to begin with; living in this kind of poverty was nothing new to us. It had always made me very proud to be able to support my mother. Even in these dire and dangerous circumstances, I found ways to bring some food into the house. I often suspected she knew that I was taking chances and perhaps behaving in a manipulative way. I avoided eye contact, but just like my sister, my mother had that sixth sense. One had to take risks just to survive. Without doing anything illegal, I tried my utmost to hold on to our dignity and to keep us alive.

As the summer of 1942 came to a close, the Germans were applying pressure on the *Judenrat* to put together a list of people who, in their minds, served no purpose. This list was to comprise the poorest and sickest people. Those people were to be transported out of Boryslaw. Sadly, not much is different nowadays. Those with wealth are the power brokers, but not to the point of being able to make decisions that bring down the hands of death.

When I went to sleep on September 2, 1942, I had no idea that my mother and I would be on that very large list of people scheduled to leave Boryslaw in the next few days. At 4 a.m. on September 3, 1942, I was awakened by a fierce banging on the door. When I answered it, a German and a Ukrainian guard told me that my mother and I were to be relocated. There was that word: relocated. Of all the lies ever told, this surely must be one of the worst. There were rumors about this 'relocation' and what it actually meant going around.

I walked alongside my mother and many other people, our suitcases and whatever food we could carry in hand, to the train station. My poor, sweet mother, whose health had been faltering for years, was further weakened by the constant hunger. She was only 58 years old, but seemed so much older. With my arm around her, I did my best to keep her upright and moving. A young man I barely knew supported her on the other side. I had to be strong and present an impenetrable front for my mother's sake. I worried about how she would handle the trip. She was already so frail.

On we walked, with the chill in the air stinging our cheeks and hands. Before I knew it had happened, my mother collapsed. I stopped to help her up, the barbaric guards shouting: "Mach schnell!" They picked her up and put her on a truck. There was nothing I could do but tell myself that I would meet her at the station.

When I finally got there, the first thing I saw were the cattle cars. Cattle cars? Were animal transports going to be used to transport human beings? My mother was nowhere to be seen. I looked around and yelled: "Yochevet Brodt? Yochevet Brodt? Has anyone seen my mother?" "No, Henek," someone said. "We have not seen her." I looked everywhere, but could not find her. It was as if she had vanished altogether, had never existed at all. There was no time to search, they were already barking orders at us: "Schnell, schnell! Line up! Line up!"

At the train station stood three German officials, including a Gestapo instructing the soldiers to keep us in line. By this time, I had a fairly good understanding of what was being said. I was waiting to board the cattle car. It was that one-way trip to death in Belzec, the one that ended in the gas chamber. The Gestapo tapped me on the shoulder and asked me my age. Instinctively I added a few years. With a simple wave of his hand, I was out of the line for the train. Just like that, I had been spared. But for what?

"You are young and healthy," he said. "You can work. You stay here." It was much later that I learned that there was a Gestapo in Boryslaw that tried to save as many Jews as possible. Was it him who waved me out of the line? I don't know, but I suspect there is a strong possibility.

I watched my friends and neighbors board the cattle cars, numb and disoriented, but did not see my mother. Inside the cars, the human cargo was packed tightly. The deportation took over a day and half to complete. The destination of this largest transport out of Boryslaw and Drohobycz was Belzec, the first of the Nazi extermination camps created for the purpose of eliminating Polish Jewry. We soon discovered that Belzec's sole purpose was the systematic murder of those who were 'relocated'. Their destination all along had been death.

In the beginning, mothers, fathers, grandmothers, grandfathers, and children were gassed in rooms where carbon monoxide was piped in. There was not even the facade of a shower. Death was slow and painful.

After my reprieve from certain death, I came back to Boryslaw, now utterly alone. I returned to our home, hoping that there was some chance my mother had been taken there to recuperate. After all, that would have been the humane thing to do with someone so sick. As I entered our house, there was a quiet that I had never experienced before. It was not just the absence of sound, it was a sick, awful feeling. This house was not only empty of human life, but there was an oppressive, cold sensation that reached into the corners of our small dwelling. This house was no longer a home. The love that had lived inside those four walls had created the warmth of a true home. That warmth was my mother, my sweet, loving mother. Now that she was gone, so was my reason for staying there. I left, never to return.

My sister and her husband, Simcha Wald, were in hiding in a hospital just beyond the ghetto. She had forged papers and was living as a Christian in a non-Jewish area. She was working, taking care of sick people, even though she was actually a beautician.

When she left, we made a promise that until this madness was over we would not contact one another. As we assured each other of our mutual love, my mother and I hoped that my sweet sister and her husband would be safe. As the son at home, I had assumed all responsibilities for my mother. How was it that I had not been one step ahead this fatal time?

I was now alone. Internally I was fighting a conflict. Deep down I suspected I would never see my mother again, but I continued to deny it in my heart. It was the only way I could survive, to hold on to the thinnest strand of hope. Or was it denial? One thing I do know is that the other side of denial is hope. Regardless, it was all I had at the time to sustain me.

I went to the office of the *Judenrat*. Exhausted, I climbed on a desk and slept. This went on for about six weeks. I remained in the ghetto working odd jobs until my circumstances changed. I worked as much as possible to keep my mind occupied and off of not being able to find my mother, although I knew on some level that she was no longer where anyone would ever be able to find her. If the ability to work was going to be the yardstick for who was allowed to live, then I knew that my mother was no longer alive. My mind jumped to all of the able-bodied people who had disappeared, and who were now supposedly dead. What sense did that make? I could not keep my mind from running from one dead end to another. It was as if I were trapped in a maze with no exit.

My work varied. I dug ditches. I cleaned streets. I even cleaned offices and was a messenger from time to time. I no longer had any family in my life. I was on my own. There was no one left to care whether I was taken off the street, sent away, or killed. No one knew that a Henek Brodt was once a law-abiding citizen of Boryslaw, Poland.

In 1943, as the ghetto was getting smaller and smaller, I was sent to do forced labor. It was shortly before July 15, 1943, when Boryslaw was declared a place to be *Judenrein* or "free of Jews." Up until that time I was sleeping in a forced labor camp near Boryslaw.

There were three forced labor camps near and around Boryslaw and Drohobycz. I ended up in the one named Mraznica. The commander of this camp was a sadist named Friedrich Hildebrand.[4] He was in charge of the Galicia area around Drohobycz and Boryslaw. He may have been the commander, but his real occupation was murderer. I would later find out that being sadistic was the primary prerequisite of employment in that position. He killed people for absolutely no reason at all.

If the inmates had family with money, they could bribe anyone to get them out. There were no morals amongst guards, whether they were German, Polish or Ukrainian. Even in these unimaginable circumstances, money talked. However, the buyout was not permanent and not a guarantee of anything at all. Even people who were able to buy their way out one day could be picked off the street at the next *Aktion*. I had no such family. Even if I had anyone still around, we were so poor that we could not have even dreamed of a so-called buyout.

The barracks in the forced labor camp were different from what I would later see in the concentration camps. They consisted of a large brick building with many rooms with wooden racks that were used for sleeping. However, there was adequate space between one another. I had a straw mattress and a blanket to myself.

In Mraznica I did odd jobs. The most tolerable of these was being a messenger. This was done according to a honor system. They knew I would be back even if I stayed away overnight which initially I was allowed to. Very few people would help a Jewish person for fear of punishment of death so my choices were limited as to where I could go. Many even joined the hate-mongering. Cries of "*Scheiss Jude! Judenschwein!*" were not uncommon. Sometimes it was easier for people to join in even the most atrocious behavior than it was to fight it. I am not excusing their behavior. People were afraid.

By this time, I was insulated. Or maybe I was just numb to the pain and humiliation of it all. Words were not hurting me. I had already been dealt a crushing blow by the loss of my mother. It was only going to get worse going forward. The things I saw people do in those days brought my faith in humanity to an all-time low. It was impossible to comprehend, and equally impossible to ignore.

I had my own job as part of the resistance. Since I could move about freely, I grabbed the opportunity to assist others. I was told whom to meet and led them safely to a place where they could go into hiding. In these dark times I was able to find some solace in helping a family keep a loved one alive. I split my time fulfilling my messenger duties and taking others to safety once darkness fell.

One time an elderly man died while in hiding. While racked with sadness, his family feared that the smell of the decomposing body might reveal their hiding place. I had to figure out a way of removing the body without being caught. I was able to organize a horse-drawn wagon and take the body to be buried. As I removed the body I promised the family that I would say a prayer, and I was true to my word.

One day I was asked by the German guard at Mraznica to go to the pharmacy in town to pick up several prescriptions and bring them back to the labor camp. Whenever I was going into town, I was to bring food from the camp to the jail where they were holding "stragglers." Stragglers were people accused of a crime, or those who had yet to be transferred to a labor or concentration camp upon the dissolution of the ghetto. These people were both Jewish and non-Jewish. Their prison guards were mainly Ukrainian.

When I entered the cells to deliver the food, I was surrounded by people shoving items into my pockets: jewelry, gold, and silver coins. All things that should have been turned in long ago. As I went to the pharmacy, I was contemplating how to get these valuables into the camp and to the rightful owners. I picked up the medication, drafted a plan, and hoped for the best.

I never gave any of the guards or police any reason to notice me. I managed to stay under the radar. When I look back now, I cannot believe the chances I took. But I returned to the camp each time without a problem. I visited the family members and each knew what item was theirs. Their hope was to bribe the upper echelon of our guards to buy temporary freedom for their loved ones.

As a messenger I also had to deliver items within the labor camp. There was a German guard whose name I am no longer sure of, but I believe it was Nimitz. He was in charge of the Ukrainian guards. Officer Nimitz's wife wanted a homemade cake from the kitchen. Arrangements were made and I was summoned by one of the Ukrainian guards and told to pick up the cake and deliver it to Officer Nimitz's wife. With threats of being clubbed if the cake did not arrive safely, I set out on my mission. Officer Nimitz thanked me but noticed a bruise on my arm. I immediately changed the subject. Explaining my injury could mean more trouble. I knew my place in this world run by the Nazis.

Numerous times I found myself being chosen to deliver items to Officer Nimitz who appeared somewhat protective of me. It seemed that the Ukrainian guards did not go out of their way to harass me. One day Officer Nimitz informed me that in the near future the camp would be surrounded and liquidated, and told me to take a jacket and pair of boots and walk out to the south of the camp. "What about you?" I queried. Officer Nimitz replied, "I will look the other way." This situation never occurred as I was moved out of this camp beforehand.

Life was predictably wretched in this forced labor camp. People were beaten for no reason other than being Jewish. Plans of escape were common. A group of young fellows, aged 18-24, were planning their exodus to freedom. I was faced with the decision to join them or stay put. Escape was always on my mind; however, I was young. I did not feel this was the time to escape. My intuition and the sixth sense that runs through my family had guided me throughout my life, and this situation was no different. I reluctantly decided to stay. The reality of the situation was that Jews were hated and no one would offer any assistance. Adhering to the unspoken code to maintain silence that had been part of my life since the orphanage, I said a silent prayer for my townspeople that their escape would be successful.

One thing that has always irked me was someone saying that a person looks Jewish. I still do not know what Jewish looks like. I had blonde hair with light eyes and was repeatedly told I did not look Jewish. For some uncanny reason the Polish and Ukrainian people could spot a Jewish person with ease.

The group of friends made an agreement that they would go into the forest and move towards the eastern front. They all agreed and made an unbreakable vow that during this escape no matter who they might run into, they would have to kill them. After all, they had all had family members murdered by the Nazis and Ukrainians. The farmers and peasants collected their rewards for turning in a Jew. The group agreed this was their only path towards life.

Once they made their escape, they could not have been out for more than a day or two when they ran into a woodsman in the forest. It was apparent that this woodsman recognized them as escaped Jewish prisoners. They were ready to stand by their agreement – they would have to kill him. But there was a problem. None of these young men were criminals, let alone murderers. Their only crime was being Jewish. So as the woodsman pleaded for his life, crying that he had a wife and children and swearing on the Bible that he would never tell that he had seen them, the prisoners listened and paused. The young men talked amongst themselves and agreed that his words sounded sincere. He even gave them his food for their journey to freedom. They let the woodsman go.

The following day they were rewarded for being upstanding and caring human beings. They were surrounded by the Gestapo, with the woodsman pointing them out. One of my friends was able to escape, returning to the camp to tell us the story. The Polish and Ukrainian hatred of the Jews had made a mockery of an act of mercy.

At Mraznica, I was with other young men my age from my town. I had a few friends with whom I would talk. My best friend and distant relative Abe was also a prisoner, although we were not in the same barrack. Abe and I would stay lifelong friends. We had both suffered losses by this point and offered one another the support one would expect from a friend and relative. Another young man was named Leon Ettinger. I kept an eye on him and he on me. Leon walked around with the weight of the world on his shoulders. He was trying so hard to protect his mother. He found someone he thought was a righteous man, a forester who agreed to hide his mother for money that would be paid on a monthly basis. Leon kept his agreement and made his payments promptly. But the forester's wife did not want to be hiding a Jewess. It was a risk, one that she probably never wanted to take in the first place. Early on one would receive monetary rewards for turning in a Jew, but hiding a Jewish person could also result in death. Leon learned that the forester's wife had gone to the police and turned in his mother. In spite of all his efforts to keep her safe, she was killed on the spot.

What could I say to Leon to ease his pain? What could anyone of us say to the other? Leon wanted revenge and the need for it consumed him. In a blind rage, he murdered the forester. His wife, knowing what Leon looked like, waited by the gates of Mraznica as the prisoners marched to their jobs. For over three weeks, we all helped to hide Leon. This was not an easy task, but many of us watched out for our own townspeople. A few weeks passed and Leon needed to get back to labor. Thinking that enough time had gone by, he took his chance. However, the forester's wife immediately recognized him, the man from whom she had gladly accepted money. One of the SS assigned to Mraznica grabbed Leon and took him away.

When we returned to the forced labor camp after work, we were summoned to the Appellplatz [place of roll call]. We were forced to watch as the SS man beat Leon to death with a truncheon. I was sick to my stomach, with a pain searing my heart and soul. Another friend and I slowly made our way back to the barracks, saying the Mourner's Kaddish for Leon Ettinger and his mother. Leon was another human being trying to protect his mother, and now they were both dead.

Abe and I were heartbroken to have to say such a painful goodbye to one of our own, however that would not be my only goodbye. Without any warning, Abe was selected to be transferred to a forced labor camp outside of Lvov. This camp was known to be horrible and dangerous.

A MOTHER'S INTUITION

On one of my many trips into town, I stopped at a German butcher shop. The man behind the counter always acknowledged my presence and was very courteous. He treated me with the same kindness and dignity that he had before the Nazis took over. As he slipped me some meat and bread, he let me know that my sister Faiga and her husband had had a baby girl several months earlier. My sister had an uncanny ability to sense things to come. Her intuition led her to believe that harm could come to their beloved infant daughter in the very near future. In order to save her life, she and her husband placed the infant in a trunk and left her by the gate of a Christian orphanage in Boryslaw. I learned that the adopted parents changed my niece's name to Adelle Bramska. Bramma is Polish for "gate." As he began to tell me about the adoption, the Gestapo came in and his demeanor immediately changed. That was my cue to leave in order to protect him.

Several weeks passed and I learned about the first mass murder in our town. Hundreds of people had been forced to dig a mass grave. Then they were stripped of their clothing and shot to death by the Nazi SS.

One day, as I was once again visiting the butcher shop on messenger duty, the man behind the counter handed me some food. He told me that my sister was among those who had been killed in the mass shooting. A Polish woman had betrayed my dear Faiga, earning a few Deutschmarks by turning in a Jewess. In addition to the money, this woman helped herself to Faiga's coat. My sister had a very unique coat that spoke not only of her profession as a beautician, but also captured her creative spirit. As I turned, I saw a woman wearing that very coat. I looked at the butcher who gave me a knowing nod. Something in me snapped and I went after her. I was in a blind rage, seeking revenge for my sister, for everything that had happened to my family, and for everything that was still happening, for every betrayal, for every death. As I pursued her, out of the corner of my eye I saw the Gestapo man heading towards me. This snapped me back to reality, and my thoughts of revenge receded in an instant, or at least for the moment. In some ways, I am grateful for his presence that day, as I am able to say that I have never killed another human being. Even in the most intense anger I could ever imagine, I did not lose my humanity.

My sister, who was known for her intuition, probably suspected that something was coming. The Nazis' treatment of infants and children was well known. She made the ultimate sacrifice to keep her child alive. We were never able to find her. Perhaps that was the best thing for her.

While I was on one of my many trips into town, I learned that my brother had been severely wounded fighting in the Russian army, and that his condition was grave. Coming into town did not always result in getting accurate information. As the labor camp was preparing to close and the Drohobycz and Boryslaw areas were declared *Judenrein*, I left with only bits and pieces of information about my family, small fragments to keep me going, if only barely. But there was so much more I still did not know.

PLASZOW

In April 1944, after working for two years under the Nazis doing forced labor, I had come to terms with the realization that my beloved mother was gone for good. I knew that my sister had been slaughtered in the first mass murder in Boryslaw. I wanted justice for the horrific deaths of my family. I wanted justice for my never-ending hunger. I wanted revenge for every lash and curse that fell on my body. My hope and spirit were wearing thin, and a horrible question was taking shape before my eyes: what was there for me beyond my family?

One day I was told to report to the cinema with my belongings and then, without warning, I was thrown onto a cattle car, destination unknown. At this point, I knew all too well what the Nazis were capable of, and what the destination might be. We were no longer calling those who spoke of gas chambers and crematoriums crazy. As we were stuffed into train cars not even fit for animals, I had no idea whether I was going to my immediate death or would be subjected to more of what was essentially an agonizingly slow death. The doors slammed shut and we were pressed together into one huge, stinking mass, body to body. People were crying, praying, and screaming. There was no such thing as normal conversation.

As so many of us were so young, I was surprised to see an elderly man, or he seemed elderly, though perhaps in his 40s. He was terribly skinny. I remembered him from forced labor and the cruelty he had to endure. I tried to make room for him, even letting him lean on me to ease his burden. We were not vermin. I had had much taken from me, so, so much, but I was relieved to find that I still had a spark of compassion left in me.

The train went down the tracks, stopping briefly in Drohobycz, apparently to pick up more human cargo. As the train rattled down the tracks, the noise it made seemed to say, death – death – death. But in my mind and heart, it sang, life – life – life. I was doing what I could to hold on to whatever hope I could find, wherever and however I could find it. Inside of me burned a desire to live. I owed it to my parents, sister and brother.

The train finally came to a stop. We were greeted with the usual: "*Schnell! Schnell!*" and were beaten by men in striped uniforms, the SS and anyone else who wanted to participate in this casual brutality. I tried to help others off the train. We were stiff from standing with so little room. When my eyes adjusted to the light, I could see that we were in Plaszow, a southern suburb of Krakow. [5]

What an odd place! I looked around and saw tombstones, blocks of cement with Hebrew writing. There were broken stones on the ground as well. It finally hit me: we were in or near the old Jewish cemetery of Krakow, which seemed fitting. The labor camp had been erected on the grounds of two former Jewish cemeteries. If I died here, at least I might have some dignity of resting in what once was and would always be holy territory for many.

Prior to my arrival in 1944, Plaszow had been designated as a forced labor camp. As the ghetto of Krakow was being declared

Judenrein, those who were not taken to Belzec (where they would be put to death) ended up in forced labor at Plaszow.

This camp included several factories and what was once a beautiful hill, where those who lived in the city could take a picnic lunch and enjoy a sliver of countryside in the midst of their city. Those days certainly seemed remote now. The Nazi commander and his assistant completely destroyed the serenity of that hill. Inmates and resistance fighters were taken to that hill to be shot and buried. Those people killed in Plaszow were also buried on this hill. It was named by the prisoners after Amon Goeth's assistant Albert Hujar, given the name Hujowa Gorka. It was not an honor naming the hill after this man, as the name refers to him as a 'penis', or its vulgar vernacular.

Amon Goeth (1908-1946) was the commandant of Plaszow until September 13, 1944.[6] Goeth was not only insane, but a sadist. He found joy in killing. His house stood on another hill, high above the camp, from where he would randomly shoot prisoners going about their business. He walked around with guard dogs and without any provocation would order them to rip a prisoner to shreds. Goeth hosted parties, having his own selection of cooks and musicians from the ranks of prisoners.

When the smell of decomposing bodies could no longer be ignored, there was a visit from some Berlin officials. All bodies buried on the hill were to be exhumed. This of course became a work detail. After the bodies were exhumed, they were set ablaze. Hitler's henchmen hoped that all incriminating evidence had now been erased, proof of the horrible crimes literally going up in smoke.

When I arrived in Plaszow, I soon discovered that there were no rules to play by. The commander was crazy; I would see a man standing one minute and then see him shot dead the next. I had no idea what to think. I could not see a guard anywhere near him. I looked toward the hill, where there was a house. My eye caught a man standing on the balcony with a gun. It was Goeth. I had no idea what the poor man in Goeth's crosshairs had done as he dropped dead. It did not matter. It was just Goeth's way, using innocent people for target practice. This particular shooting happened within a few minutes after we got off the train and were marched to the showers.

It was at this point that something jumped into my brain. I was becoming increasingly proficient at communicating in the German language. It was similar to Yiddish, which is gentler than the German's hard and guttural language. With each passing day it seemed that my command of the German language was improving. Through the years I became fluent in German, and acquired fluency in several other languages.

Plaszow, German concentration camp near Krakow Poland (first published in Poland before March 1st, 1989 without copyright notice) – from wikimedia.org

NUMBER 12891

After leaving the train, we were put into rows of five. From that point onward, it was five by five. In those columns of five, we marched to the showers. As we were marching, we saw our suitcases being carted off in carriages drawn by horses. When we arrived at the showers, we were stripped of our clothing and sent off with a small piece of soap. This soap had an odd odor to it. The water was ice cold and when we came out we were sprayed with an industrial-strength substance, supposedly to get rid of lice. We were then shaved allover. It did not bother me until I saw some of the young women on the other side of the fence rubbing their heads, crying over the loss of their dignity. It was, especially for them, an utterly degrading experience. As if this were not dehumanizing enough, we also had to give up our identities. Yes, we were stripped of our very names. We were now literally just numbers. I was no longer a human being named Henek. I was, very simply, number 12891.

Along with my new identity, I was no longer allowed to wear civilian clothing. I was given a striped uniform made of rough, thin material. There were pants, a shirt, and a cap. I was given shoes that were little more than pieces of wood with a plastic strap. Yet looking around I saw many people without shoes. I made a mental note to protect my shoes.

As we walked, I felt awkward and uncomfortable in my new striped uniform. The uniforms, unsurprisingly, were not well made or adapted to size. The barracks had wooden racks approximately seventy-five feet long and thirty-five feet wide, with three rows on each side. We were to sleep on these hard boards. Some had blankets, some not. What I learned that first night was that I would share my rag of a blanket with two other people. Just outside the barracks were the latrines. We were each given a red tin bowl and spoon. I made a belt out of string to hold up the pants of my ill-fitting uniform. The string also served as a means of tethering my tin cup, which would hold the "food and liquids," what little we received of either. At times this bowl might hold some water so I could wash myself. I slowly sharpened the other side of my spoon. If we were lucky enough to get jam with our bread, I wanted to be able to spread it. I held on to these objects with all of my might, as these were my only means of survival.

I learned early on to hang on tightly to what I had. My newly assigned wooden clogs became my pillow. I was in the barracks with people from all over Europe. There were French, Russian, Greek, Dutch, and Norwegian people. In charge of each block was a Blockalteste who made sure the barracks were cleaned, handed out bread, and ensured we made it to the Appellplatz. Those who were chosen to be Blockalteste were not nice. Like so many others, they thought they were safe by doing the Nazis' bidding. They were no better than the Jewish police had been. They sold their souls to the devil. We learned that in order to survive, we had to stay on good terms with the Blockalteste. I did my best to maintain a low profile, just blending in as best as I could and not causing any trouble.

Work was under the supervision of so-called kapos. A kapo was also a prisoner. Some were political, some were murderers, and some were Jews. The color of the triangle on their uniforms defined their status. In general, one did better on a work detail with a political prisoner as opposed to a sadistic criminal. I was identified by a Star of David.

It was in Plaszow that I learned to organize. By this, I do not mean keeping my very few belongings neat. We would organize extra food and the little things that we needed. Essentially, we worked with others to obtain those things we needed to survive, day by day, minute by minute. In some ways organizing was stealing. The Germans took all of our belongings. In a manner of speaking we worked with others to get some of the essentials back.

Food was scarce. Each morning we were given a very dry slice of bread fortified with sawdust. There was a liquid that they called coffee, but it bore no resemblance to coffee or anything else we had ever tasted. Later in the day, we got soup that had nothing identifiable in it. We were lucky to get between 400-600 calories a day. What I came to discover was that there was a standard cookbook shared amongst the concentration, labor and death camps. It was amazing that the coffee and soup were the same every day and in every camp, whether in Poland, Austria or Germany. So we tried to organize more food. The fact that I had been a messenger for the Jewish council in the ghetto was worthless in the Nazis' eyes. However, I still got to be a messenger from time to time. Every now and then we would be rewarded for hard work by being given cigarettes. This was a coveted commodity. I would trade cigarettes for bread, as I was not a smoker. Organizing was essential to keep me from becoming a Muselmann, the term for people so emaciated, worn out and detached from reality that they were essentially the walking dead.

In Plaszow, I did some manual labor as well. I was not a tailor and had no real trade. Manual labor could be anything from digging ditches to carting away dead bodies. I made sure I said the Mourner's Kaddish very quietly for those poor souls who had met their demise. I was fully aware that the person in the cart was someone's son or father.

Days started early in Plaszow. We were woken up at 5 a.m., sent to the latrines, and then summoned for roll call. Under the kapos' watchful eyes, I performed various tasks of manual labor every day, except for those days when I went into town for special work.

It was not easy getting by. I knew a few of the other men from Boryslaw and Drohobycz as well as those I had met at the forced labor camp. Each of us had our own heartbreaking stories. Although we did not think we had enough room or energy for compassion, oddly enough we did. Many of us were in similar situations. We did not have the luxury of forming a brotherhood. It took everything we had just to stay alive.

Throughout my journey in the camps I encountered people that I knew from my hometown. It was good to see a familiar face. What happened had profoundly changed us. We were no longer the same. It was best to always keep conversations shallow. Where are you from? Are you alone? You never knew whom to trust. People do things when they are fighting for their life that they would not otherwise do. I protected myself the best I could while not losing sight of that I might need to offer assistance and that I might need help.

I did not want to become like the kapos. I had a moral compass and cared for others. By being compassionate I had survived life in the orphanage. I made a silent pledge that whenever possible I would offer assistance and do whatever I could to make life a little better for my fellow human beings, although I was determined not to lose myself in this ordeal, no matter what. I was aware that I had to come first in order to survive.

The nights were the hardest. Sleeping was difficult. While I had shared a room with many others at the orphanage, this was different. Crying, babbling and praying could be heard all night long. We were crowded and could not turn easily to get comfortable. Irritation was common amongst us. The three tiers made it challenging if someone had to use the latrines. It was usually *verboten* [forbidden] anyway once the lights were out.

ONE DAY AT PLASZOW

It started like every other day in Plaszow. We were rudely awakened by the typical screams of: "*Schnell, schnell!* Move, you *Scheissjuden!*" However, there was a distinct feeling in the air, a chill that went to my very core. It was a feeling of profound dread.

A word was being whispered from one person to another: selection. The number of people in the camp had risen to almost 20,000. There were people from all across Europe. It was difficult to have a conversation when so many of us were speaking in different languages. Yet somehow we were able to communicate. For many, Plaszow was the first stop. Many of the more "experienced residents" felt that we needed to guide the new ones to keep them as safe as one could be under such desperate circumstances.

As we guided the newer inmates toward we knew not what, we went to the selection. Most of us had learned enough by then to know that selection was not going to be a good thing. We were forced to strip naked and parade by a few German officers, and at times, on their request, do calisthenics so that they could make the decision whether we were fit enough to live.

As if this situation was not stressful and dehumanizing enough, this bizarre selection process was done to music. While I do not know the composer or even all of the words, it went something like this: "Everything will pass by and flowers will bloom again in May." It was a surreal experience, like some exhibition in hell.

Once again, fate stepped in to save me. When my turn came, with the simple wave of a riding crop, I was sent to my right. Just like that, I was granted yet another reprieve. I had survived another day. Haunting me for life is the group of segregated people. Cries and screams could be heard. It was clear that friends and loved ones were torn apart.

Despite the inner turmoil of selection and segregation, life went on.

CHILDREN IN PLASZOW

I could not believe my ears when one of my hometown friends told me this story about Plaszow. I heard it when I had already left that place. He told me that when the ghetto was emptied, those who still had families brought their children to Plaszow. I did a double take. Children in hell! However, I had never seen a child in Plaszow. According to my friend, people were promised that the children would be well cared for while they worked. There was even a special area for the children. It was a group of small barracks with a playground that was fenced in. I shook my head as he continued to tell the story. I was stunned. As I searched my memory, months after leaving Plaszow, I never saw the special area, playground or children.

By this time most of us knew that we could not believe anything the Nazis told us, but those parents believed that their children would be safe. Everything was a cruel joke. While the adults were kept busy with work, everything came to a standstill. Music was piped out of the loudspeakers, however this time it was a different type of music. There was an unexpected roll call, which left everyone asking why. That count seemed to go on forever while the music played. Without the usual fanfare they were released from the count, and my friend suddenly heard screams and crying. The children were rounded up and placed on trucks and taken away from their parents. It was not until much later that my friend learned that these innocent children had been put on a transport to Auschwitz to be murdered immediately. I was numb and yet I could not deny what my friend was telling me. Why would he make this up? From what I knew of Nazi tactics, this seemed to fit the pattern. Now I know that this indeed happened.

I later found out that Amon Goeth was under investigation for stealing money from the Third Reich. Maybe this was his way of trying to get back in the good graces, by sending those incapable of working to their deaths. This probably included that first large selection and the dismantling of the children's camp. From the Nazis' perspective, children and the elderly were just a drain on the German economy.

When I was in Plazsow I heard rumors of children living there. However, as my friend unloaded his emotional burden onto me, I knew this would be one of many stories locked in the vault of my memory of how cruelly the Nazis treated children and how little respect they had for the family unit. The desperation of being unable to protect one's wife or child. Hearing this story I was consumed by rage. I could not have cared less about the work I did. It was nothing more than a means of channeling my anger. There had to be justice. Sometimes, that thought was all I had to hold on to. It was all that any of us had. I was in hell.

After the war I testified against Amon Goeth at the Dachau trials. Goeth was sentenced to death.

Amon Goeth as prisoner (August 29, 1945), first
published outside of the United States, before
March 1, 1989 without copyright notice, from
Wikipedia.org

WIELICZKA

I stayed in Plaszow for about four months, leaving in mid-June for a subcamp called Wieliczka. Wieliczka was originally a salt mine but had been turned into a concentration camp shortly before my arrival. It is frequently linked to Auschwitz, though it is about 65 kilometers away. Like Auschwitz, it was a death camp.

During the Nazi regime, several thousands of Jews were transported from the forced labor camps in Plaszow and Mielec to Wieliczka. By the time Wieliczka served as a concentration camp, the salt the town was known for had already been mined. The Germans used their slave labor to build an underground compound, where they planned to manufacture plane parts and ammunition. The Nazis were quite adept at hiding their evil intentions from the world.

In many ways, Wieliczka was no different from Plaszow. The barracks were similar. The hierarchy was the same. Each barrack had a Blockalteste and every work detail had a kapo. In terms of basic structure and operation, life here was nearly identical: hell.

The work was in a hillside cave, and therefore a little bit cooler than being out in the summer air. We were worked well beyond the point of exhaustion. Many died as slaves toiling to build this plant that would facilitate more death and destruction. We were fed very little. Each day I felt the hunger and thirst more acutely. The work may have been different, but the cruelty and sadism were the same.

I tried hard not to lose my faith in God. I often wondered when He would lead us out of this hell. What could we have done to be treated so cruelly? It was at this point that my religious instruction from my early days in the orphanage came back to me. It was as if God began to answer my questions and prayers. As I was digging to build the Germans a factory so they could convince themselves that their dreams of world domination would soon be realized, I began to focus my thoughts on a higher power. It was never our place to question God but to put our trust and faith in him. Human beings were given free will. I was certainly a part of something larger than myself. I had to have faith and I reminded myself never to lose my sense of humanity. This was instilled in me by my mother and it was the code I lived by in the orphanage. If I could offer help to someone less fortunate, then I needed to do just that. I could only honor my mother's memory by doing the right thing. Faith became even more important to me.

I promised myself that I would look out for others, resisting all of the games that pitted one of us against another. I was catapulted back in time to the orphanage when I had to stand strong, although for different reasons. I reminded myself that I made a commitment to live, perhaps as the only surviving member of my family. I watched out for myself and others. To give the guards and kapos no excuse to beat me, I dug and reinforced the wall for the German's factory of hell and at the same time I reinforced a much stronger wall around myself, a fortress of faith and hope.

At the end of the working day, we came out of the mines in our lines of five. I will never forget when my line of five included a corpse. There were of course countless corpses, but on this particular day and this specific occasion, there was one in my line of five. Dead or alive we had to be in our row of five.

The Germans were fastidious about numbers. No matter what, the same number of workers who went into the cave had to come out, even if one of the workers was dead. The principle of five by five should be maintained under all circumstances. We were always in our same five. We returned to the barracks, and were "rewarded" with something that resembled soup. It was barely enough to keep us alive. I had learned early on that it was best to not be in the beginning of the food line. Solids such as meat and vegetables were more likely to end up in your bowl as you got to the bottom of the cauldron. Sleep came easier for me those nights, since I had finally made my peace with God. Neither the cries and moans nor stench of hard-worked bodies kept me awake.

THE FRONT COMES CLOSER

As the war continued, we had no news as to what was actually happening. It was hard to hang on to hope when there seemed to be no end in sight. This had been commonplace since the beginning of the war, but more so since entering the camps. Being a slave, starved and mistreated was becoming the norm. Would it ever end? We did not have access to newspapers or radios. It had been forbidden for a Jew to own a radio for a long time. We never had one, so we never felt its loss.

The status of the war could be told from the mood of the German officers. The worse the Germans were doing, the crueler they were. There was less food, if that was even possible, when the war was not going in Germany's favor. I came to realize that the worse sensation was that of thirst. Given a choice I would rather have my thirst quenched than have something to eat. However, I did not have a choice!

At some point it became clear that the Germans were losing. The officers were enraged, forcing us to work longer hours. The soup, meant to keep us alive, no longer held any traces of nutrients and appeared to be filthy water. Even waiting near the back of the line served little purpose. How were we to survive this?

My time at Wieliczka was very short. Thankfully I never saw the completion of the underground compound. I am not sure if it was even completed. Information was shared by newcomers that the Russians were gaining ground and that it was time for us to move further away. One thing was for certain, the move was not in any way related to our safety. We were never given any information about what was going on, where we were going, or why. We were just told to line up. Of course that meant in fives.

JOURNEY TO MAUTHAUSEN

The day we were pushed and beaten towards the railway tracks was hotter than any day I had experienced up until that point or since. The train comprised cattle cars linked together. We were shoved and packed into these cars. Just when you thought not a crumb could be squeezed in, they managed to load more human cargo onto my car. Cars that should have held no more than 80 people, or 60 cattle, were carrying at a minimum 130 people per car. We figured out a way to make it work, sitting one on top of the other, side to side, and front to back. There were men of all nationalities, religion and ages. It was not long before people were crying out, suffering from an unquenchable thirst. As hungry as we were, our only thoughts in the cattle car were of water.

In an effort to find out where we were being taken, we hoisted a man up to a very small, screened opening, the only vent that let air into the car, to look for clues. It appeared that we were leaving Poland, but we could only speculate about where we were going.

Every so often the train would stop. It was at one of these stops that our cries for water were finally heard. In retrospect I believe that this was the only time I had received water during transports. I hadn't let go of my rusty red cup, which now seemed to be amongst my most precious possessions. Next to me sat an old man, maybe 50 years old. It was rare to see a man of this age, especially one in such bad shape, alive. For all I knew he could have been younger, these circumstances have a way of aging the body. He was trembling, drifting in and out of consciousness, as his head rested against my body. I wondered whether he might actually be in a better a place, nearly any other reality had to be better than this one. He had no cup, and therefore was not given his ration of water. I took the end of my shirt and dipped into the little bit I had and wiped his face to bring him at least some small comfort. Like every other victim of this nightmare, he was someone's father, someone's brother, someone's son. I held his head in my arm and gave him some of my water. He began to come around and looked up at me questioningly. "Warum?" [Why?] I did not know what he was questioning. Our situation? Our mode of transportation? I had nothing to say, other than urging him to take a little more water. I was young and in better shape. I didn't have much left, but I shared with him what I could. When we disembarked from the train I did not want him to be a corpse in my line of five. I also wanted to remain the son my mother would recognize. That was all I had left to give her. For the remainder of this trip, I became this man's self-appointed caregiver.

The train continued down the track until one of the passengers spotted a sign and called out to the rest of us. We were now in Austria. It must have been a day later. Once again, the music of the train going down the track, death – death – death, stopped. Our cattle car, along with the others, came to a halt. The doors opened, and soldiers with guns in hand had us in their sights immediately. The message was clear: Don't you dare move, not an inch. Next to our train, on a parallel track, was a military transport. Their train looked nothing like ours. Through the open doors, we heard the yells of the Gestapo: "Throw the dead out of the car."

Those words became etched into my brain. These dead were people, human beings, or had been before they became a pile of bodies to be disposed of. They mattered deeply to someone, somewhere. It broke my heart to hear those heartless words. Everything our faith holds sacred, little by little, the Nazis desecrated. In our faith, the handling of the body of the deceased is done through a very specific and precise ritual. The Nazis made a mockery of us, even in death. As the dead bodies were taken out, sobs could be heard along with the groans of discomfort.

In the meantime, the heat of the August sun continued to bear down relentlessly. If there had been water in the compartment, it would have boiled and the moans of thirst only grew in intensity and desperation. It reached a point where I could no longer trust my own eyes or ears. A high-ranking Wehrmacht soldier walked up to the SS in charge of our car and pointed out our clear distress and thirst. "Can't you hear the people crying?" he said. "Can't you give them some water?" Unfazed, the Gestapo simply asked the soldier if he would like to join them. With that, we watched our hope for relief walk away. The officers' exchange was an eye-opener for me. There were at least a few righteous souls left in this hell. Not every German soldier was evil.

ARBEIT MACHT FREI. MAUTHAUSEN

Without any food or water for the passengers, our train kept moving, and the awful music continued to play as we rolled down the tracks: thirst – thirst – thirst – death – death – death. Finally, the train stopped for the last time, and the familiar cries of "*Schnell! Schnell!*" once again pierced the air. I always tried to get out of the cattle car amongst the first. It was likely that I would then not be beaten as severely. "*Mach schnell! Mach schnell!*" We had arrived in Linz, Austria. In our usual formation we marched several kilometers to the next camp. We were worn out, yet we tried to physically support the ones who were growing weaker by the second. We continued to be prisoners of the Third Reich and were now prisoners of the Mauthausen concentration camp.

Everywhere I turned, people were speaking different languages. I saw people from Hungary and was immediately struck by the relative girth of their bodies. War had seemingly not taken the same toll on them as it had on my Polish brethren. Many Hungarians I saw seemed to have been spared the impact of antisemitism. The Jews must perhaps have been protected longer.

I got the impression that we would not be at Mauthausen for long. It seemed to function more as a supply house of human beings. The Angels of Death, or physicians, would check us out in the most dehumanizing way possible to see whether we still had the ability to work. If not, we would be murdered. In Mauthausen, there were gas chambers and a means to dispose of the bodies. Furnaces seemed to shoot flames into the sky. The Nazis continued hiding their crimes by cremating the murdered. It was possible to kill 80 people at one time in the gas chamber. The crematoriums were the workhorses of every concentration camp. Upon arrival there was a hum in the air. I could make out cries, babbling and screams. My eyes watered, and there was the sweet acrid smell that comes with the burning of flesh. I will never be able to erase that smell from my mind, no matter how long I live.

Once again, we marched in our groups of five to be registered. I was given a new identity: number 84503. We were then taken to the showers. I no longer had any belongings with the exception of my cup, spoon and shoes that the officers could lie about returning to me. I was simply dispatched to the shower without any pretense. When I was done showering, there were no towels, but the air was so hot that we dried quickly. Despite the shower I did not feel clean because of the stench. To the tune of *"Mach schnell! Mach schnell!"* we were marched naked, five by five, to have our heads shaved yet again. We were sprayed with a disinfecting liquid that stung my recently shaved body. I could not understand why this was happening. What made us different from other human beings? There was some talk about the Aryan race. Strange, I had light hair and light eyes, typical of many Polish people. This was insanity. I remained lost in my thoughts, yet also acutely aware of my surroundings, so that I could blend in outside the barracks. My survival depended on it.

The barracks were larger than those I remembered from the last camp. There was no straw, just the unyielding hardness of the wood. The hierarchy was the same. Once again, we had to endure the casual cruelties of the Blockältester, those delusional fools in charge of the barracks who had convinced themselves that their allegiance to the Nazis would exempt them from the fate the rest of us faced.

I claimed my area to sleep and could not believe my eyes when I saw my dear friend, Jurek, from home! Finally a familiar face in the insanity. Jurek slept next to me, my shoes forming a pillow under my head as usual.

WORK IN MAUTHAUSEN

I awoke to the sounds of sticks hitting the barracks and someone shouting: *"Raus, raus! Schnell, schnell!"* It was morning already. I could not believe it but someone had stolen my shoes. Neither Jurek nor I heard or saw it happen. I had no choice but to help myself to another pair of shoes from a dear soul who no longer had the need for them. Despite him being dead, I still struggled with the guilt of using his shoes. At 5 a.m. we moved to the latrines. It did not take long, as we were not given enough liquids to generate much more than a trickle of urine. It was the same routine as always: five by five, *"Schnell, schnell!"* with the usual expletives. All of us were accounted for, including those lucky enough to die during the night.

I was in line to get an even smaller piece of bread and some light brown liquid. I ate quickly and was too hungry to even consider saving a piece for later. I grabbed for Jurek, hoping that we could try to exchange a few words about home. He told me that his mother was taken to Belzec and that he suspected she had been killed. Jurek informed me that the sole purpose of Belzec was murder. I nodded knowingly as my breath was sucked out of my very body. Who knew how many of us shared this same story? As it turned out, Jurek had spent some time fighting in the resistance. We whispered to one another, forming a pact that at the next opportunity we would try to escape. We were well aware that an attempt to escape would be enough to get us killed. Then again, doing nothing was enough to get us killed. What was the difference?

The SS guards were splitting us into groups for a work detail. Along with their shouts came hitting and pushing: "*Scheissjuden! Hund!* Over there! Over there!" The kapo led our group into a stone quarry. I could not believe my eyes. This was not an ordinary work detail, not the typical slave labor to support the Nazi war effort. This work was designed specifically to kill us, to work us to death.

We were to pick up a boulder, climb 154 (although research indicates that there were 186 steps, I am sure there were 154) steps to the top, drop the boulder, and then walk back down. The oppressive heat made this work nearly impossible. We were beaten and cursed at as we toiled. I heard a scream and saw a man topple off the top, along with his boulder. He had been pushed by a guard for no apparent reason. Laughs from the other guards echoed in the quarry. The full magnitude of this work detail finally registered with me: they were going to kill us without needing to waste any bullets. We were just a conveyor belt delivering corpses. That was the work. That was what we were here to produce, our own dead bodies. I heard my mother's voice in my head, encouraging me to keep going: "You must live, Henek."

One of my memories from Mauthausen that stays with me to this day has to do with the suicides that I witnessed, helpless and frozen in place. Men would throw themselves at the electric fence or hang themselves in the barrack. These human beings had lost all hope. Death seemed better than living under those conditions. We had no notion of when or even if this ordeal would ever end. For them, death was an escape from the torture of living. All I could do was renew my promise to survive and remember my humanity toward others.

Climbing up with a heavy boulder only to drop it off at the top was permanently etched into my body and soul that day. By the end of the first day, we had lost more than 20 souls. Jurek and I were chosen to bring back one of the deceased. As always, we had to maintain our five by five formations, and we had to return with the same number of people we started out with. When I turned to Jurek, he looked as if he had aged twenty years.

By the time we got back to camp, the population had grown. The new people brought with them good news regarding the war: Germany was losing. The Nazi soldiers were now dying by the thousands. Finally, we had something to celebrate, some tangible reason to continue to hope and hold on. My stay in Mauthausen was short lived as I had suspected. I was there somewhere between six and ten days. The camp population was bursting at the seams, and I was soon transported to my next location.

Prisoners in Mauthausen © Bundesarchiv, Image
192-269 / CC-BY-SA 3.0
http://creativecommons.org/licenses/by-
sa/3.0/de/deed.en), via Wikimedia Commons

MELK

Once again in the cattle car, we were transported to outside of Melk, which is about 60 kilometers from Vienna. By now, I was becoming more accustomed to traveling like this than I would have ever been able to imagine. We were treated like animals – worse than animals actually – so it makes kind of sense that we traveled in cars designed for animals. At least the weather was becoming cooler. Nevertheless, we were hot, hungry, thirsty, and tired. We marched five by five approximately 5 kilometers to the Melk concentration camp. Those of us who were still alive had developed a completely different, and sadly distorted, concept of normal.

There were fewer and fewer people from home. With each move, we were introduced to different people. In some circumstances the only thing we had in common was that we were Jewish. Others were just deemed undesirable by the so-called superior race. In this crime alone, we were united, branded, and condemned.

As we arrived at Melk, I prepared myself for the routine I had learned from repeated experience: get out and off the train as quickly as possible to avoid the blows from the soldiers and bites from the dogs. I looked around me and got together a group of five. As long as the Germans were in charge, we needed to march five by five.

We took turns giving our number, which remained the same from Mauthausen. I was still 84503. That was all I was as far as they were concerned. Number 84503, property of the Nazi regime. Five by five, we marched off to the showers. It was at that point that I noticed a few familiar faces from my hometown.

Once again, we were shaved, sprayed with that same stinging disinfectant, and given a new uniform. It was the same striped type of uniform as before. Rather than receiving my dirty uniform back, I got to wear someone else's dirty uniform. I could not see the logic in that, but what difference did it make? There was no point in applying logic to anything anymore. The next stop was to be branded. One of the prisoners, soft-spoken, told me to give my arm. On my wrist was tattooed KL. KL stood for *Konzentrationslager* [concentration camp].

It is against Jewish law to have a tattoo. This was yet another way they degraded and decimated our belief system. The message was clear that our place was on par with cattle, or probably lower. I would later learn that Auschwitz was the only concentration camp to tattoo numbers onto prisoners' forearms. As I walked on in both shock and anger, I put my wrist up to my mouth and sucked out the ink. I would continue to do this throughout the days that followed. I would be damned if I would be branded. This had nothing to do with my religion, human beings are not to be branded. At this point in time I was ready to live or die, and take my chance to escape. KL on my wrist would stigmatize me a prisoner. Also going through my head was that I wanted to survive and tell the world what happened to the Jews of Europe. I would not go through life with a tattoo. Nowadays, I have a very small telltale sign on my wrist. It is not noticeable unless I point it out, and even then you have to look very closely.

When I had my chance, I made my way over to two men from home. I was happy and relieved to see familiar faces. In my group we were down to three, so we grabbed two brothers to complete our five. Now we were ready to march to the barracks. Once again, they looked the same: wooden planks employed for maximum capacity. I saw a few blankets but not enough for everyone. Sleep proved to be challenging as we were packed in one on top of the other. At night it was the usual moans, screams and coughing. I was shocked by my own body odor and the smell of those around me. Would I ever feel clean again?

The structure was the same as always. There were kapos for work and Blockältester. I don't remember the name of our Blockalteste, but I had learned that these people were fairly predictable.

Once again, we were awakened very early, quickly getting out of bed to go to the latrines, the only place where there was any heat. I had learned at this point to hold on very closely to my tin cup and utensils. Without them, I would not be able to eat at all.

After roll call, we ate: the same pitiful menu consisting of bread made out of sawdust, some unidentifiable liquid that might have been coffee or tea, depending on your ability and willingness to awaken your imagination. Can one imagine that this liquid is a thick chicken soup served to welcome in the Shabbat? No, it is hard to imagine when your entire body is working is in fight-or-flight mode.

Then came a series of instructions, each shouted: "Hurry, hurry! Eat, eat! Line up for work! March out!" I had no idea what we were going to be doing. Eventually, I learned that we would be going into caves to yet another well-hidden factory to manufacture ammunition and plane parts. We were hidden away from surveillance so the German war machine could keep turning. We were back to doing labor for "the cause."

As I surveyed my new working environment, I noticed that we had kapos supervising us, as well as civilian workers. Most of the civilian workers were no better than the kapos, guards, and the SS soldiers in terms of how they treated us. It seemed that regardless of who was in charge, our lives and working conditions were equally dire. One of the kapos rose to power when he was released from prison for murder, which was indicated by his triangle, while another's badge reflected his status as a non-violent offender, perhaps a traitor to the Third Reich. His demeanor was a bit softer.

In this camp, many people lost their lives to the occasional caving in of sand, most likely due to the lack of training and expertise. There were no engineers on hand with the knowledge or experience to fortify these underground plants and make the working conditions safe. Certainly the Nazis did not care, as long as ammunition and plane parts were being produced at a satisfactory rate.

Newly arrived prisoners are assembled in the Appellplatz (roll call area) at the Melk concentration camp © United States Holocaust Memorial Museum, National Archives and Records Administration, College Park, photographer unknown, 1944-45

WORK UNDERGROUND

"*Raus! Schnell, schnell!*" One morning faded into the next. Up again before dawn, to the latrines to grab a moment's warmth, and then off to the Appellplatz. We stood in line for bread and "coffee." That particular morning we received a special treat: a smear to spread on the bread. I cannot recall whether it was margarine, cheese or jam. All I knew was that it was different, life-saving calories perhaps. A fleeting thought went through my head. I hoped this extra treat did not mean the war was going well for the Nazis. We ate quickly and got into our formation of five, reporting to the kapo in charge of our work.

Our task for the day involved building an underground tunnel. One of my friends got my attention by pointing to some empty bags of cement. Before I knew it, he grabbed one for each of us. Others had already discovered the bags' purpose: insulation. I remember thinking that despite the gaunt faces, others who worked with us appeared a bit heavier. Before we knew it, the empty bags were gone and our thin prison garments padded out. Our clothing served only to cover our bodies. We had no other protection from the unforgiving elements: no jackets, gloves, hats, or boots. I still had clogs, but no socks to go with them. Now, with a little ingenuity and good luck, we had insulation against the freezing temperatures and bitter winds of the Austrian mountains.

We were worked hard in this camp. The food was as bad as always. We were hungry, thirsty, tired and weak, and were eaten alive by bed bugs and lice. There was yet another danger facing us: dysentery. Besides the weakness and imbalance of electrolytes that comes from chronic diarrhea, we were further dehumanized as neither the kapo nor any of the civilian workers gave us any time to step out to relieve ourselves, despite the onset of this serious illness. We had no choice but to "go" where we stood, never stopping our work. After all, we were working for the war effort, and the Germans, who were growing increasingly desperate, needed all the help they could get.

Cave-ins were not at all uncommon. However, on one particular occasion, the weight of the sand caused the conveyor belt to break. There was nothing that anyone could do. This conveyor belt was essential to our work. Without it, we were unable to continue, so all we could do was sit and await orders. This was an unusual occurrence. The civilian's first response before checking on the well-being of us humans was to figure out how to repair it. We were reported to the guards as if it was our fault that the belt had broken.

Out of the numerous times I was assaulted this day stays with me, and yes, that is the term, assaulted. When human beings are punched, hit with clubs or whipped, it is assault. Whether or not it was our fault that the conveyor broke did not matter. It was if that one broken belt caused Germany's slide into defeat. I was beaten so savagely and repeatedly that I was in pain for weeks. This was the worst I was ever beaten. Having grown up in an orphanage where corporal punishment was commonplace, I was numb until that point to the constant hitting and whipping while I was working. But this beating took my breath away with the sheer magnitude of its savagery. This time I was not alone, but part of a group. I had to witness the ferocity of the beatings administered to my co-workers, knowing that I would soon be beaten in this very same fashion. Fifteen vicious lashes on my bare back. How demeaning to be whipped without clothing on your back.

After that beating, we were moved to another area to continue working until roll call. We returned to camp to carry out the same routine: roll call at the Appellplatz, the barracks, the food rations, and the hard wooden planks that served as beds.

Sleep was difficult that night. We were on top of each other with many having significant stomach and bowel issues. Crying, moaning, scratching and screaming pierced the quiet of the night. The stench was overwhelming given the lack of time and materials for adequate human grooming and hygiene combined with the diarrhea staining our clothing. Everyone was at the end of their rope. There was no way for us to cooperate and help one another. I was grateful that at least I had a hometown friend with whom I could commiserate. Our friendship was becoming increasingly important for both of us.

THE HORROR CONTINUES

We were told it was forbidden to use cement bags underneath our uniforms. "They slow you down," we were told. If anyone was found with a cement bag under his clothing, the punishment was death.

It was a tough decision. I could wear the cement bag and be warm, facing an instant death if I was discovered, which would at least be an end to this perpetual misery, or I could be cold and continue to die in excruciatingly slow increments. I chose to remove my bag. One young man from my hometown chose to keep wearing his, a life or death decision.

A second threat was made that if the camp population did not deal with this offender, they would segregate the Jews into their own barracks. The camp population consisted of human beings that were undesirable in the warped mind of the Nazis. There were Jehovah's witnesses, Greeks, Italians, mentally disabled and Jews. Political prisoners and murderers were also common. I think the prison population was predominantly Jewish, however within our barracks there was diversity. Surely, a barrack of only Jews would result in more abuse.

They sent the young man from barrack to barrack to be dealt with by the inmates. By the time he made it through half of them, he was taken away and never heard from again.

Sadly, this corrective strategy was fairly common. At the discretion of the German overseers, certain prisoners were singled out to be beaten to death by the others. Some were murdered in their sleep, while others were sent from barrack to barrack, where they were beaten until they were dead. It occurred to me that these same people, under different circumstances, would have never thought to hurt another person. They robbed us of our possessions, our families, our dignity, and our lives. They were robbing us of our humanity as well. I decided that I would not participate in this horror show for the Nazis. There were many others who also followed this mode of thinking.

Shortly after that incident, while I was working underground, one of the sand mountains gave way. Work in that area stopped until our party was joined by others. Side by side, we toiled until the end of the day. As all the work groups lined up in the customary five by five for roll call, we were short by three men. We were counted and recounted, but no matter how it was done, my group remained short by three men.

This count and recount went on for hours. We were exhausted and hungry. The night was slowly turning into day. One of the kapos asked the other if, when the sand collapsed, he had performed a count to make sure that all of his workers were accounted for. That question was, in turn, quickly posed to the civilian workers. A casual shrug of the shoulders revealed how little compassion they had for the missing workers, all certainly dead. Once again, we were reminded of just how dispensable and insignificant we were.

At last, the three men were found buried in the sand, dead. Now the numbers matched and order had been restored. The search for the missing men had consumed the entire night and part of the morning. There was no return to camp for us. Five by five, we went back to work without sleep or food.

HUMANITY WITHIN THE BARBED WIRE

We continued our backbreaking work, with a woeful lack of food and medical care. Hunger and thirst prevailed. Dysentery became increasingly common. We did not have calendars or any way of knowing what day or month it was. The cold, rain and snow gave us some sense of the time of year. There seemed no end in sight.

Not surprisingly, suicide was common. We were given strict instructions: "If Jews want to commit suicide, let them. We are running out of bullets."

One incident from my time in Melk stands out. It was meal time. A friend from home had received his bread. Suffering from severe diarrhea and its side effects, he remembered the standard home remedy: toast! He went into the latrines, the only place with heat generated by a flame, and attempted to toast his bread. The Blockalteste caught him and took his bread away, giving it to another prisoner in our barracks.

At the orphanage I had learned that if someone was punished by losing a meal, that person would eat better than the rest of us because we would each give that child a piece of our own food.

While I thought about my friend, the recipient of that extra piece of bread came up to me and gave me the bread to return to him. Unable to find my friend, I walked into the barracks calling his name several times. I saw a shadow and said, "What is the matter with you? Why don't you answer when someone calls your name?"

As I walked closer, I saw that he was hanging by his belt from one of the upper tiers of the bunks. Without wasting a minute, I used the other side of my spoon, the one I had sharpened, to cut him down. I was relieved to see that he was still breathing. I did not blame or judge him, knowing there was only so much one human being can take. When the Blockalteste came in inquiring about all the noise, I told him what had occurred. His only response was: "Where did you get the knife?"

As I recall, we were eventually able to organize some medicine to help my friend with his severe case of dysentery. The man who had returned the bread had shown great constraint as well as compassion. We were starving and one extra piece of bread could make a difference. There was an unwritten rule that you never ate another person's bread. The circumstances, horrifying as they were, did not change my friend and nor had it robbed him of his humanity. I wish I could say the same for the Blockalteste.

CONVERSATION WITH A GERMAN OFFICER

One day, a German officer stopped me to ask a question. I immediately took off my hat, my eyes cast down.

"Who are you?" he asked me.

"I am a Polish Jew," I replied.

"Where were you born?"

"I was born in Poland."

"So, you are Polish?" he asked.

"No sir, I am a Polish Jew," I said.

We went back and forth like this for a while, and I could feel my ire building, though I was, of course, careful to maintain my composure. Finally, I asked him if I could ask him a question of my own.

To this he responded angrily, "How dare you ask a question of a German officer of the Third Reich!" Nevertheless, he granted me a question.

I tried to choose my words carefully, but there was something I had been longing to understand from the beginning of this ordeal, and I saw this as a chance to articulate the essential question. "I am Polish," I said. "I have committed no crime other than being Jewish. Why am I here?"

There it was, at last. Out of my heart, out of my mouth, and into the open. Why was I here? Why were any of us here? Why was this happening to us? There was an awkward silence, and then a moment passed between us. The officer turned and walked away without uttering a single word. I considered this a triumph and I knew that this brief conversation was enough to get me killed. Maybe it was my imagination, but I like to think that he had some internal struggle with what Germany was doing, and his part in that cause.

I came to realize that not all Germans were Nazis. People were afraid. A German soldier never knew who was around him. Who was a true follower? Who swore allegiance to Hitler? Perhaps that German officer believed the propaganda, perhaps not. However, for the length of a conversation, this German officer was perhaps trying to make sense of the insanity in his own way.

DEATH MARCH

It was April 19, 1945, and spring was beginning to reveal its glories in the Austrian mountains. Flowers blossomed, green returned to the trees, and birds flew freely. We remained in the same hell, of course, but there was something about spring that brought us hope of new beginnings, and despite my situation, I began to sense that things were about to change.

The front was moving closer, and we were to be evacuated from Melk. My cup and eating utensils, which were secured to my belt seemed to grow heavier each day as we marched to the Danube River. We were put on boats, which took us down river. In any other circumstance, one might have marveled in the beauty of our surroundings.

Once we got off the boat, we marched in our five by five columns for three full days without food or water. I could not even imagine the sight we must have made as the front was coming closer to us on three sides.

Those too frail to keep up were shot on the spot. With each mile, we were stepping on and over bodies, which, as far as the Nazis were concerned, were just more obstacles on the trail. Gun shots were common. If someone looked near death, or was too weak to walk, the Germans opted for the bullet.

Without enough time to rest our bodies, which were fatigued and beaten down beyond description, our five by five became our only support. We helped one another as best we could, quietly changing positions so that we could hold up the weakest of the five. We knew this ordeal would soon come to an end, one way or another.

During this march, I heard the voices of my mother and sister encouraging me to carry on: "Keep going, you must live." Their words, their voices, became my driving force. I prayed to God to give me the strength to endure. God answered my prayers and I made it to the next destination: Ebensee.

Aerial view of the Ebensee concentration camp © United States Holocaust Memorial Museum, courtesy of Gisela Wortman, May, 1st 1945

EBENSEE

I could not believe my eyes. As I walked through the gate of the Ebensee camp in Austria, the combination of smells and sights was almost too much to bear. I scanned the sky as the smoke billowed, suffusing the clouds with the ashes of more innocent victims. I thought of the souls ascending into heaven. Who were they? Where were they from? Does anyone know that they were here? That awful smell of burning bodies, that terrible, sweet smell that screamed death of the innocents brought me back to reality. The stench seemed to stay inside my nose and course through my blood. It seemed to permeate every pore, every cell of my body.

I was in the midst of the demise of Europe's Jewish population. In this camp surrounded by beautiful Austrian mountains, bodies were piled up everywhere, some horribly bloated, others decimated that the bones could be counted like matchsticks. In one corner stood a mountain of human hair. Hair that would be stuffed into a German's family mattress so that they had a layer of softness beneath them. A woman's crowning glory sheared off for the comfort of the master race.

Chimneys stretched into the sky, working day and night, emitting what remained of the victims into the air. Again, I thought of the families or whatever might be left of them, denied the practice of their faith in the traditional burial customs.

The Ebensee camp seemed to be bursting at the seams. It was built to house 7,000- 8,000 people. However, there seemed to be approximately three times that amount. It was crowded with both the living and the dead. The barracks had been built to house 100 people each, but they were occupied by closer to 700 people. It was obvious to us right away that we would be sleeping on the floor, if we were to sleep at all.

When we walked at night, it was impossible to tell if we were stepping on the ground or on human bodies. It galled me when the guards had the audacity to cover their faces with a handkerchief. After all, they were accomplices in the deaths of each and every one of these victims, who were now nothing more to them than an offense to their senses.

By some estimates, there were 350 people dying every day. Some died due to the hard work. Others died at the hands of the Nazis and guards of various backgrounds. The non-German guards came from several countries across Europe, including but not limited to Ukraine, Poland and Lithuania. What they all had in common were prejudice and hatred towards different human beings. Regardless of the manner of death, there was no question who was responsible.

The tiny amount of food we were given was yet another sign that the Nazis were losing the war. Work details no longer related to the German war effort. My work consisted almost entirely of loading bodies onto carts. When no one was looking, I whispered the Mourner's Kaddish. I did not know if these people had anyone alive to say it for them. It was my duty as a Jewish man to pray for those who no longer walked the earth. It did not take too long before others joined me. As I prayed, my thoughts were always with my own family, my mother, sister, brother, and brother-in-law. I also had my three half-sisters, and I had no idea what had become of them.

In an effort to dispose of the bodies and the smell, those in charge came up with a quicker, more efficient means: the digging of mass graves. The Germans then poured lime and water into the crater, and many bodies were buried in this manner.

We did not feel the same urgency the Germans felt. As they were getting ready to flee, they tried to cover their tracks in every way they could. It was clear that the guards were preoccupied, almost frantic, as the days wore on and their defeat drew nearer. Despite all the efforts to bury and cremate the bodies, the piles continued to multiply.

The Ebensee prisoners had to construct enormous underground tunnels in which armament works were to be housed. Working conditions were inhumane. We continued to persevere day by day, with an astonishing lack of food or water to sustain us. I organized what I could, as I did not want to be a Muselmann. One could feel it in the air that things were changing rapidly. We all knew the war was closing in on Germany. If only we could hang on a bit longer.

View of the crematorium in Ebensee © United States Holocaust
Memorial Museum, courtesy of Lillian Pressman, May, 1st 1945

BEGINNING OF THE END. THE TOWER OF BABEL

We knew in Ebensee that things were not going well for the Germans. Throughout April 1945, the food continued to dwindle. There were fewer young SS guards. The Wehrmacht army, composed of what looked like older soldiers, many of whom also fought in World War I, were now working as guards. Some were not as harsh as their predecessors had been, but we still understood quite clearly that we were prisoners. One day we heard strange sounds, the steady hums of an aircraft. The ground literally rumbled and shook with the dropping of bombs. The combination of this blissful noise and the warmer weather of spring gave us a sense of hope despite the never-ending smoke and that sickening sweet smell that continued to pour out of the chimneys.

Meanwhile, the population of Ebensee continued to grow, as did the piles of bodies. I wondered where they were all coming from. Sickness and starvation continued to claim many lives, as did the gas chambers and bullets from the SS guards' guns. As April turned into May, the crematoriums still could not keep up and bodies continued to accumulate in massive heaps, limbs horrifically tangled.

On May 6, we were called to assemble at the place of roll call. The camp commander spoke to us, seemingly wanting to ensure our safety from the Allies' bomb raids. All I could think was that they were concerned for their own safety. Anyone of them could shoot us as easily as they buttoned their jackets. He demanded that we move into the nearby caves in the Austrian Alps surrounding the camp, where we would be safe from falling bombs.

We stood still, refusing to comply as word spread from one language to the next that the caves were mined. The Nazis continued to try everything they could to eliminate the evidence of their monstrous crimes. But we had heard the warnings, held our ground and were staying right where we were. We did not mind going back to our barracks, but we refused to go into the caves.

There was no work that day, and I took some time to take a good look around at all of my condemned brothers. We were Jewish, Christian, Jehovah's Witnesses. What we had in common was that we were all enemies of the Third Reich. As my eyes moved from one person to the next, I saw that some were sickly, others were Muselmänner. Most stood there with blank stares. The majority were little more than walking skeletons. Many no longer possessed a full set of clothing. Some just had uniform shirts, others had only pants. Sickness was pervasive. For some, despite their grave appearance, there was still a detectable fire in their eyes. It was the fire of resistance, a burning desire to stay alive.

Later that day, we heard some strange noises. Along with others I ran outside to see what the commotion was all about. I was shocked to see tanks rolling into Ebensee. What was this? Were they reinforcements from the German military? As I squinted to see into the distance, I realized that these were tanks with white stars. This was something that neither I nor others around me recognized. We knew that Russian military vehicles carried a red star, but which country had a white star? Trucks, cars and soldiers began to march in, and at last I saw red, white, and blue, the bright colors of the

American flag! Yes, the white star on the Sherman tanks was the white star of freedom. Was it possible that liberation was here?

Soon I heard it with my own ears: "You are now free." We could hardly believe what we were hearing, and yet there was no mistaking the message. We had been liberated by the powerful and infamous 80th division (702 3rd Army 80th division) of the United States Army.[7]

As I looked at the United States soldiers, many had tears running down their faces, overcome by the magnitude of suffering and cruelty they were witnessing. Some stood as if in shock. There were dead bodies everywhere, many piled high, most of them naked.

Desperate survivors had taken their clothes and shoes. That is what we had been reduced to in order to survive. The American soldiers saw the widespread starvation and promised us food. We were cautioned that we should eat slowly. Sadly not everyone was able to take that advice. Many literally ate themselves to death.

Now the tables had turned. The treatment by the Blockältester and kapos had been beyond unacceptable. They had been treating us as no human being should treat any living creature. At the time of our liberation, a group of prisoners turned on a kapo who was infamous for his cruelty, beating and stabbing him to death. In the midst of this sudden violent outburst, several American soldiers tried to step in, pleading with the recently liberated victims to allow the legal process to take its course. "But where was the legal system for us or our families, who were all murdered in cold blood?" someone asked the soldiers. What could they possibly say? They stepped aside and never said another word. A rush of thoughts went through my head. On some level I knew this was wrong, however the manner in which we had been treated was unspeakable.

I turned my head in another direction, just in time to see a German soldier surrendering his weapon and dog. Near him stood several liberated men. Not one person turned on him, as he was known as an individual who tried his best to treat all of us with dignity and respect. The recently liberated stood near him as if to protect him from violence from those who were not as familiar with his gentle nature.

I was only 19 years old and knew with certainty that my mother, sister, and brother-in-law had all died at the hands of the Nazis. I had also heard that there was a strong possibility that my half-sisters and their families who all lived in Warsaw were among the dead. I was not sure about my brother, but I was not hopeful.

I began to sob. We were free, but I did not know where I would go or to whom I could turn. Suddenly, the weight of being alone in the world pressed down on me. I was an orphan again. I had lost years of my life, years during which I could have learned a trade, or could have courted a young lady. I realized I had grown up fast.

Poland was no longer an option for me. At one point I was proud to be a Polish citizen. However, Poland and her people had turned on us at every corner. Poland held nothing but misery for me. My home and family were taken, where would life lead me?

LIFE GOES ON

I remained in the camp for a bit longer. I watched as the American government forced the German and Austrian people to come into the camp and see for themselves what this so-called master race had done to fellow human beings. The previous agents of our misery were forced to dig graves for the bodies that remained. I struggled with that, as even in our liberation, the dead were still denied their Jewish rites of burial. Where was their family? Still in prison uniform, I walked almost daily in procession to bury our dead.

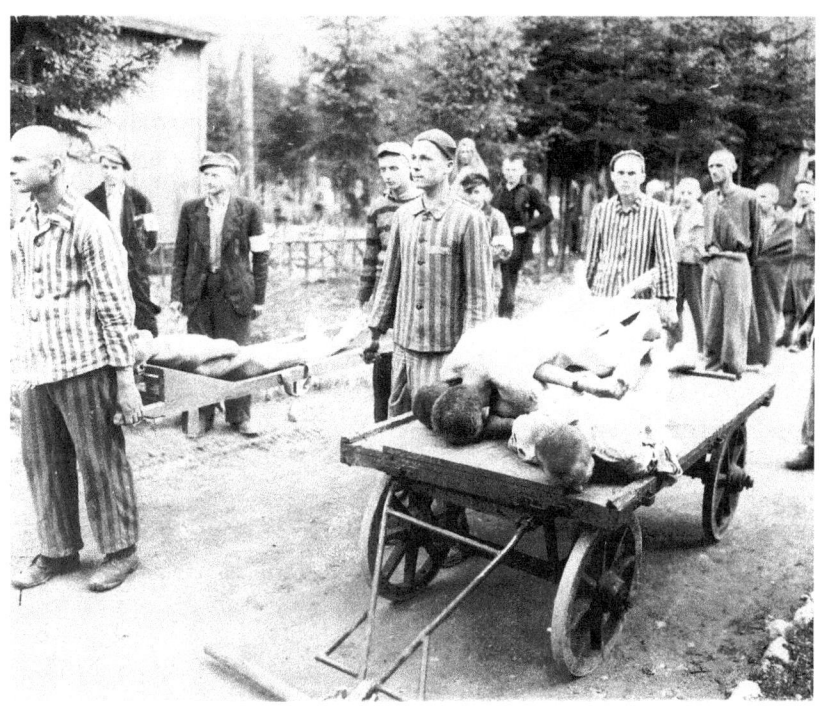

Survivors wearing their camp uniforms remove the dead on carts and stretchers at the newly liberated Ebensee concentration camp, May 7, 1945. Hank Brodt is standing sixth from the left, partially obscured, wearing a prisoners uniform, cap and armband © United States Holocaust Memorial Museum, courtesy of Arnold E. Samuelson

For those that were Jewish, I said Kaddish as numbers now paired with names were called out and the bodies that had been attached to them were placed in the ground. I also said Kaddish for my mother and my sister. For once I was able to chant the prayer loudly, because there was no one nearby ready to whip me for my faith.

The United States military did all they could to make the concentration camp better for us, addressing the needs of tens of thousands of survivors. The Red Cross came, along with medical care for those in need. The military built showers so that we could wash away the years and layers of filth. No matter how long I stayed in the shower, the sorrow and trauma could not be washed away. I had to wear my uniform until the military arranged for civilian clothing. For the first time in years I was treated like a human being. I was greeted politely by a smile or a shake of the hand.

It was clear that from May 6, 1945 I was indebted to the United States of America for getting me back on my feet. I was anxious to learn English. Like before, I watched and listened. But this time I tried to learn English because I wanted to, unlike the German language which I learned out of fear.

Survivors talk to American soldiers in Ebensee © United States Holocaust Memorial Museum, courtesy of Eugene S. Cohen, May 8, 1945

One day, a friend and I decided to take a walk into town. Not too far from the camp, a woman stopped me and asked if the two of us would like to join them for dinner. Initially hesitant, and understandably still suspicious of Austrian/German nationals, we talked among ourselves and decided that fear should not rule our lives any longer. We graciously accepted the invitation. I found my face turning red when our hosts told us that they had had no idea what had been happening to us in the camps. I am sure she saw the look on our faces. As diplomatically as possible I said that every single day, more than 2000 living skeletons had passed her house on their way to slave labor. How could she have missed that? How could she be making such a claim now? I walked a fine line, not wanting to insult our host, but I also did not want to enable her denial about what had happened and her complicity in it.

Austrian civilians are forced to dig graves for corpses found in Ebensee © United States Holocaust Memorial Museum, courtesy of Dennis Beck-Berman, May 8, 1945

WORK AND HOUSING

As I walked back to the camp, I saw a group of American soldiers and inquired about work. They told me they had no money to pay me, but offered me a place to stay as well as meals in exchange for work. Having had enough of the camps, I wanted to make myself as independent as possible. I was assigned kitchen duty and took great pride in my work.

Slowly, I began to learn English. There were also some Jewish soldiers, some of whom spoke a little Yiddish. We got by. I felt more at ease around a certain group who were part of a company. Another sign that we were treated as human beings: I had a choice about whom I could talk and spend time with. When that group packed up to move on to Germany, I went with them. I ended up in Wolfratshausen (near Föhrenwald in Bavaria), a former labor camp turned into a displaced persons camp by the Allies.

Group portrait of survivors from Boryslaw and Drohobycz, who have assembled at the Föhrenwald displaced persons camp to commemorate the fourth anniversary of the first pogrom in the Boryslaw-Drohobycz ghetto © United States Holocaust Memorial Museum, courtesy of George Oscar Lee, November, 6th 1946

When I arrived there, I could not have predicted what a pivotal and important role this place would play in my life. I met an American soldier, Sergeant Carl Nusbaum. Carl's family escaped Germany just as the political landscape was changing. We seemed to understand one another, and soon we became friends. Before he returned to America, Sergeant Nusbaum promised that he would send an affidavit with an invitation for me to come to the United States. I thanked him but had experienced that when people say something with noble intentions, it does not mean that they will deliver.

As I continued to work for the army, I met a lovely and lively young woman, Ruth Slome, who worked at Föhrenwald. She was recently married, yet we struck up a conversation. Ruth was from Czechoslovakia, and while her nuclear family survived, many of her other relatives had died. One day, Ruth invited me to her house for dinner. I was made to feel right at home. I met her husband Bruce, her parents... and her stunning younger sister, Kathe.

Kathe had big brown eyes that seemed to look right into my very soul. Before I realized it, and much to my surprise, I found myself telling her my story. She listened, and with eyes glistening with emotion, she reassured me that I was safe now, while praising me for my determination and resilience.

That night I returned to the base, but I could not sleep for hours, as my thoughts kept returning to the amazing woman I had met earlier and all that we had talked about. When I finally fell asleep, I dreamt of my mother. I felt as if she were in the room. In the dream, my mother was shaking me, urging me to get up and go to work. I had a wife to support. A wife?

I had no doubt at all that my mother had sent me the message that Kathe was the woman for me. The message in that dream was unmistakable, as was her presence in the room.

After the liberation and the Germany army was neutralized – although the United States did not declare an end to the war against Germany until the early 1950s – I along with others were summoned to testify in Krakow and at the Dachau trials. The tables had turned and I gave testimony against Amon Goeth, the one time commandant of Plaszow. At Dachau I was summoned to testify against SS Obersturmführer Friedrich Hildebrand (1902-1983) and others who were part of the Nazi murder campaign. I struggled mightily with the prospect of reopening wounds that had barely begun to heal, but I knew that I had an obligation to those murdered under the watch and at the whim and command of the Nazis. I held on to share with the world how hate killed my family and so many more people. In 1953 Hildebrand was given an eight-year sentence for his crimes against humanity. Eight years! I was stunned. It seemed that not much had changed.

Years later, in 1967, I received a request to come to Bremen, Germany to testify again of the crimes against humanity committed by Hildebrand and others. In court before a three-judge panel, the first question I was asked was what language I would be using to testify. By then I was American, and being proud of my country, I chose to testify in English. During my testimony, I noticed that the German interpreter did not translate my words correctly. Understanding that this distortion of my testimony could be a factor in the verdict, I corrected in German, as politely as I could. The prosecutor agreed with me. However, one of the judges stood up and angrily stated: "Can you imagine this man speaking perfect German and requesting an interpreter?"

I looked this judge straight in the eye, and with the dignity of an American, I shrugged my shoulders. I had been called here to testify. In my country, we enjoy freedom of speech. I chose English as the primary language of my country. I knew antisemitism was not dead. I just wanted to get out of there. However, justice was served. Hildebrand, surely one of the most sadistic men alive, received a life sentence for his crimes against humanity.

THE UNITED STATES

Much to my surprise, Sergeant Nusbaum kept his promise. I received the affidavit and an invitation to come to America. Carl and his wife Bernice documented their intent to sponsor and support me.

As I boarded the ship, I promised Kathe that I would keep in touch. After a few weeks at sea, accompanied by a severe bout of sea sickness, I finally arrived in New York City on March 17, 1949. I could not have been more impressed, these New Yorkers were so welcoming. A ship filled with immigrants arrived, and they had a parade. Unbelievable! I was not really that gullible, but I love telling that story as a joke. It was actually St. Patrick's Day. Even so, the contrast was not lost on me. In America, I was now in a country that actually celebrated diversity.

Hank as he sailed away to America to start his new life (March 1949)

True to their word, the Nusbaums took me into their home. As I have mentioned previously, my independence was very important to me. I arrived on Thursday March 17, 1949 and by the following Monday, I had a job as a shipping clerk which paid $30 per week. While I was grateful for their generosity, it was important to me to make my own way as soon as possible. Now that I had a job, I needed to find a place to stay. With a bit of help navigating the language issues, I found a boarding house where I paid $22 per week in rent.

I was enjoying my independence and happy to be earning money. I was trying to move forward, burying the traumatic memories of my past by leading a productive life in the present. It was vital for me to stay in the present, but this has never been easy.

During my time in New York, I ran into some of my hometown friends. They decided to move to Chicago and wanted me to join them. After a discussion with Carl and Bernice, and a great deal of soul-searching, I decided to make the move. I was a single man working hard to put down roots in the country that sacrificed so many men for our freedom. My hometown friends and I had a great deal in common, since most of us were the sole survivors of our family. We had a bond that could never be broken, one that no one else could possibly understand. How could they? We were able to keep our promise to keep in touch.

Once I arrived in Chicago, I moved into a friend's apartment. I found employment in a machine shop earning $54 per week. I was sharing the rent and was soon enjoying my new life.

GREETINGS FROM UNCLE SAM

One evening when I arrived home from work, I found a letter waiting for me. It was an official envelope from the United States government. Even though I was not yet a citizen, I had received a draft notice. I did not need to think twice. I was proud to serve in the United States of America's military. I owed more than gratitude for my freedom. This was my chance to give something back, to "pay my own way," at least in part.

I packed a suitcase and drove back to New York in order to report to Fort Hamilton. The army offered me many opportunities. I could earn my GED, as I had only attended school up to 7th grade. I also had the opportunity learn a trade. I took full advantage of this good fortune. Soon I was a high school graduate and had learned how to weld and operate a lathe.

I was drafted during the time of the Korean War, serving from October 1950 until October 14, 1952, and subsequently was in the active reserve for three more years. When I received my marching orders, all I could do was stand there in shock: I was to be stationed in Germany. I was proud to serve the country that liberated me, but overwhelmed that I had to set foot on German soil. The brass knew my situation and background, and gave me the opportunity to request a change of assignment. When I understood that assignments were based on need, I accepted it and was actually proud to return to Germany wearing the uniform of the United States Army. Of course, I had an ulterior motive as well: I had every intention of trying to rekindle my romance with Kathe.

By this point I was fluent in German, the language Kathe and her family spoke at home. Spending time with her and her family further improved my skills, which proved to be a big benefit to the army. It was not too long after World War II, and the war with Germany was only beginning to come to an official end. I was able to pass valuable information on various subjects to the brass. I renewed my romance with Kathe, and as an American soldier, I married her in August 1952. We had some rough hurdles, but we were able to cross them all. I brought my bride back to New York City.

Wedding day in Germany (August 1952)

OUR LIFE IN A NUTSHELL

Kathe adjusted well to life in America. Her sister Ruth and husband Bruce were already living in New York City. Kathe was very close to her parents, so she wrote to them on a regular basis. As an American soldier I was able to bring over many of her things to help her feel at home. Kathe, to put it simply, was brilliant. She spoke many languages, each with a native accent. She learned English from a teacher from England, so in the early days she spoke with a wonderful British accent. From the time I married Kathe, every day when I came home from work she had dinner prepared. We would talk about our hopes and dreams as a couple, trying hard not to look back.

In the years that followed, Kathe and I had two beautiful daughters. Evelyn, our eldest, married Stuart Lenoff in 1976 and had two children: Wayne and Kaitlyn. Kaitlyn married Richie Horwith in 2012, and Wayne got engaged to Miriam in July 2015 and they married in March 2016. I am happy to say that I was able to dance at each wedding and share in these blessed events.

Evy graduated from the University of Tennessee with a degree in Special Education, which permitted her to teach. She continued with her education in order to become a guidance counselor. She left the classroom and is now director of guidance in a Florida school. I would describe her as the daughter with the gift of patience.

Deb, our youngest, has always been interested in the Holocaust. She graduated from Virginia Commonwealth University with a BSW and received a Masters in Social Work from Fordham University. She is married to Dan Donnelly, a retired police lieutenant. Sadly, they were unable to have children, as Deb suffers from many autoimmune diseases. However, she and Dan enjoy spoiling a multitude of dogs. Deb enjoys her job as a social worker in an education setting, with a small private practice where she specializes in trauma.

As is the case for many mothers, Kathe's children became her world. We made a solemn promise to one another that no matter what happened, our children would come first. Kathe had goals to have a family, a house and someday an education. Through my work as a carpenter, and a number of side jobs, we were able to buy a house in the suburbs of New Jersey.

Kathe, who had been denied an education just as I had been, earned her GED, and then took a test and that, combined with her life experience, placed her at the junior level of college. She graduated summa cum laude with a degree in accounting. But Kathe did not stop there. She took the CPA exam, receiving one of the three highest scores in the state of New Jersey. At that point, she had her pick of jobs. She took a position in a small accounting firm that she loved.

But not everything was coming up roses for us. During her senior year of college, Kathe was diagnosed with stage 4 ovarian cancer. Needless to say, this was a devastating blow for us. With surgery and radiation treatment, she made it for four years until the cancer came back in her bones and within months throughout her body. There was more treatment, and Kathe fought as long and as bravely as she could before we lost her in 1978.

After 22 years of living the life of a widower, I found companionship with Aida, a Russian immigrant. In April, 2000, we were married. We left the home I had known for most of my life in the New York / New Jersey area. With my new wife, I moved to High Point / Greensboro, North Carolina. My daughters were not happy about the move, since I would no longer be living near them, but it felt right for me.

It was not an easy period of adjustment. I felt pretty isolated and lonely in the beginning. Eventually, I joined Temple Emmanuel and became friends with Rabbi Fred Guttman. The Rabbi was instrumental in getting me to share my story. In the beginning, he gave me gentle nudges, which grew more insistent as time went on. The population of survivors was dying off. This was a story that must be told, and who better to tell it than an actual witness, someone who had been able to survive the atrocities that took place in the camps? Slowly, at the Rabbi's urging and with his support, I began to reveal my history.

In 2006, I was invited to accompany a group of teens on the March of the Living, an annual event that brings people from around the world to learn about the Holocaust and its evil roots. For the first time since I left, I would be traveling back to Poland. With some understandable reservations, I finally accepted the Rabbi's invitation. Deep down, I knew that it was important to teach the younger generation about genocide by visiting the various camps. From Poland to Israel, we marched, in celebration of life, and in honor of those whose lives had been cut so tragically short.

I am happy that my relationship with my grandson Wayne has developed and grown through the March of the Living. He accompanied me twice. My granddaughter, Kaitlyn, is equally special to me. Kaitlyn is named after my deceased wife, and is the apple of my eye, as they say. In many ways, she reminds me of my younger years when both my daughters were much younger. Kaitlyn is a straight shooter; you always know where you stand with her.

I am grateful that my daughters have husbands who love them. Due to my time living in New Jersey, I have obviously spent more time with Danny. He is a true gentleman who takes good care of Deb. I admire his workmanship in building decks and all the work he does around their home. It is obvious that they have great love and respect for each other. Had circumstances been different, Danny and Deb would have been great parents. I see how they care for their dogs. Their commitment to assisting others through their respective careers speaks volumes of their characters.

My older daughter has been married since 1976. Both she and Stuart are wonderful parents. Stuart is Evy's partner in everything. Both have careers, and I have seen him do chores equally to Evy around their home. It is obvious that their children come first in their lives. They are both natural parents. It was heartwarming to watch as Evy and Stuart opened up their hearts and home to their children's spouses' family. Both Evy and Stuart work hard in their jobs in education. A well-earned retirement is in their not-so-distant future.

These days, I keep busy speaking at schools, community centers, churches, universities, military bases and civic clubs. When I am not speaking, I play tennis and go to the gym. I want my body to function as well as my mind. I am proud to be a member of the Temple Emanuel community. A few years ago when we were attending a festival, the Rabbi called me over to introduce me to an elderly gentleman, telling me that this gentleman had served in the army during World War II and had helped to liberate a concentration camp. Of course, my interest was piqued, and I asked him which camp. "Ebensee," he replied. "You liberated me!" I said. What else could I say?

For more than seven decades, the experiences I had in the camps penetrated the best defense I could muster and found their way into my consciousness. I still have nightmares, sometimes waking up on the floor. My daughter Deborah, who is a therapist, has reminded me with great compassion numerous times that although I am resilient, nightmares are not uncommon, given my history of prolonged exposure to complex trauma. Perhaps what she says is true, but that does not make them any less difficult to endure when they come.

I am often asked why I think I survived. I wish I knew the answer to that. Why I survived and others of my family did not. The Germans typically killed those that were older, grandparents, parents and disabled. I was young, healthy and able to work. Growing up in an orphanage I became what they now call street smart. I was observant and tried to stay invisible. At one point it became very important for me to live through the ordeal. I wanted to tell the world what was being done to innocent people.

THE SEARCH FOR FAMILY

Ever since the end of the war, I have been trying to find members of my family. In the early 1960s, two cousins on my father's side found me. I was shocked to learn that I still had family. I had no recollection of them, perhaps because I was so young when I last saw them. When oranges arrived from Israel, I passed them out to people in the building, celebrating the incredible news that I had family that had survived.

My daughter Deborah later on greatly assisted me in my search. We wrote to everyone possible, pursuing every path we could find. The Red Cross stepped forward, performing a tracing service of its own. Unfortunately, this turned out to be a dead end. We had several people translate letters to the Russian consulate and military in search of my brother. Again we came up empty-handed. With every year, there was another avenue opened to search for family members. Each time the result was zero.

I came to the conclusion that I was the sole survivor of my immediate family, otherwise they would have found me. I was at the point where I was ready to stop searching, as I was coming up with nothing but disappointment, but my daughter frantically continued her search. And when she has something in her mind, it is very hard to distract her. I vacillated between anger and hope as she pursued all avenues to find a trace of our family. As we would soon discover, all hope was not lost. While I was involved in the difficult task of sharing my story with a new generation, I had no idea what was happening back in New Jersey. My daughter Deborah recounts her story here:

My husband, Danny, joined me in the search for relatives. Each May we would attend Police Week in Washington, DC, paying our respects to law enforcement who died as part of the "thin blue line." Each year, we would make our way to the Holocaust Museum and go upstairs for research, but without any result.

In the late 1990s, an article appeared in the local newspaper about two cousins finding each other after the war through the website JewishGen Family Finder. I saw no harm and registered. Initially, the only response was silence. Finally, in late April of 2007, I received an inquiry from someone named Oleg. His message read as follows:

Dear Debora

I am wondering if you are any relation to Simcha, son of Nachman Brodt. If so please contact me, if not I am so sorry to bother you.

Oleg

I screamed and walked around the house in a daze. I had so much energy, I did not know what to do with myself. I never had a feeling like that in my entire life. Danny told me to answer Oleg's message cautiously. Danny, the man who always helps keep my feet firmly planted on the ground, said: "Let's wait and see." I followed his advice and answered as follows:

Dear Olga

Simcha is my father's brother and Nachman their father. Who are you?

Regards, Deb

I waited over one week for the reply. I was embarrassed that I had responded so quickly, without taking the time to check the name carefully enough to avoid turning dear Oleg into a woman named Olga.

Finally he responded and told me that he was Simcha's grandson. We corresponded for several days. I checked him out every way I could think of to ensure that he was legitimate and that this incredible revelation was authentic before I dared to tell my dad.

Pictures of Simcha and Nina that were received in 2007 to establish the relationship between Hank and Oleg

We exchanged a few pictures. I then sent a picture of Simcha to my sister Evy and maternal cousin Bernie. As my cousin opened the email, his wife Roz walked by and said: "Oh, what a nice picture of young Uncle Hank!" Bernie had to explain the miracle that was unfolding. When Oleg sent a photo of himself, all doubts were put to rest: he was the spitting image of my father at that same age.

I could hardly wait for my dad to return to America. I was thrilled with these recent developments, and eager to tell him what had transpired in his absence. When I told him the news, he immediately planned to call. That day, I was scheduled to volunteer as a crisis mental health worker following a tragedy that had resulted in the loss of life. It took great discipline to focus while I was awaiting the outcome of the transcontinental telephone conversation. "Deb, you and Oleg did it," my dad told me. For me, it was gratifying to play some part in bringing my dad's brother's family back to him.

I recently asked Oleg what inspired him to look on the Jewishgen Family Finder website. I asked him if he heard my father's name on the radio when he lit the candle in Birkenau. Oleg told me that it was not that. He and a co-worker had been talking about the Holocaust, and Oleg mentioned that his grandfather's family were assumed to be dead, except for Simcha. This young man suggested that he should post his grandfather's information on the website. If any family were still alive, they might respond. As fate would have it, when Oleg went to check out the website, there stood my long unanswered post. My number of cousins doubled. I now had four first cousins rather than two. My father quickly made plans to return to Israel to meet his brother's wife and family.

My father had no pictures of his family of origin. The few that his mother had were long gone. After he reunited with his brother's family, we discovered that they had one picture of his sister and several of his brother. He did not need any photograph to remember his beloved mother. His memory of her is as clear as it could possibly be.

Hank's brother Simcha and Nina with their beautiful twin boys
Alex and Emil

The question why Simcha never looked for my father was finally put to rest. After the war, Simcha recuperated from his wounds and returned to Boryslaw. The news he was told was very grim. Simcha learned that his younger brother was a resistance fighter who was killed, just like his wife, mother and sister. Since Boryslaw held nothing for Simcha, he left never to return to Poland. We could not find him because the Russians had changed the spelling of his name to Symcha Brodt. Simcha Brodt did not exist. Sadly Simcha died in 1986, never to know that his little brother was alive and well, living in the United States.

Hank meeting Oleg in 2007. Oleg began the email
correspondence that brought the families together.

MARCH OF THE LIVING

I participated in the March of the Living on a yearly basis from 2006. My grandson, Wayne, accompanied me twice. Wayne has a degree in recreation. He has always been a natural when it comes to working with teens. He was a chaperone on the tour, as well as my "buddy." Please note that I am still as independent as I have always been. I do not need Wayne or anyone else to take care of me. I simply enjoyed having my grandson with me.

To date I have joined the March of the Living eight times. One trip stands out for me as I deviated from the usual routine of speaking solely to our group. As we were walking through Auschwitz, a group of three young ladies asked questions to our Rabbi. Rabbi Guttman pointed me out to these lovely young ladies and suggested that they speak to me. The Rabbi encouraged me to spend as much time as needed with these tourists from Holland. This group of friends had decided to tour the concentration camps on their own. Committed to Holocaust education, I shared the history of the Holocaust as well as the role it played in my own life. They were very interested to learn as their own country was very much a part of Anne Frank's story.

The March of the Living is an integral part of a proper Jewish education. Every teen who wants to go should be able to do so, even if their family does not have the funds. It is an essential experience. I can highly recommend it.

Hank and Wayne during the March of the Living in Masada
(2013)

POSTSCRIPT – PERSONAL LETTERS AND REFLECTIONS FROM LOVED ONES

Included here are letters from Hank Brodt's daughters, granddaughter, grandson, nephews, and family friends including the Rabbi Guttman.

From Deborah Donnelly, youngest daughter

This is a story about my father, a Holocaust survivor. While this is one man's story, during that very dark period in time across the world, there are many people (perhaps even the daughter of an American soldier) who have their own stories to tell. It is incomprehensible to me how one man's ideology – and all that followed from that – could wreak havoc across several continents and bring such great loss to so many families.

Across the United States of America, many young men volunteered to fight to maintain our freedoms and prevent Hitler from carrying out his promise, or threat, to come to the United States. Many joined the armed forces having some knowledge of Hitler's Final Solution.

One man's story could not be told without the sacrifice of so many Americans. Death and despair came knocking at many doors during that time period. I cannot imagine a mother's cry when she learned that her son met his demise on the beaches of Normandy or a young daughter who would never see her daddy again after his death on a European battlefield. Those empty hearts that cannot be consoled – their souls' wounds were caused by one madman.

While it is very painful for me to hear about my father's life under the Nazis, I am grateful and proud beyond words that so many Americans willingly put themselves in harm's way to defeat the Nazi ideology. I express my deep and heartfelt condolences to every family who lost a family member in the pursuit of freedom. I thank each and every family who had a family member fight during World War II. They saw firsthand the horrors of war. In addition to that exposure, there were many soldiers who liberated the concentration camps and to this day still have nightmares about what they witnessed. It changed many lives forever.

Their family history and mine will forever be intertwined. To those of you who liberated Ebensee, and to your family members, I thank you from the bottom of my heart. Without the valiant efforts of those soldiers, I and many others would not be here.

As this book is brought to fruition, it is important for me to share that my father is so much more than a Holocaust survivor. He is known in his Jewish community as a survivor. To my sister and me, he is so much more. Many years ago, it was set in stone that his family came first. There was no greater gift than family. My father enjoyed time with his children and their mother. When my mother met an untimely death, my father was the glue that held the family together. As we grew up, my father would do anything to ensure that we did not go without. Despite long working hours, he always had time to read to me. It was my father who taught me to tell time. Many years later, he was the one who taught me to drive. What *would I have done without his cry of, "Look out, the man opened his car door!" "Gosh, Dad, do you mean the guy four blocks down?"*

My father had patience. He was never one to throw caution to the wind.

I do not have to dig deep to find memories of my father that make me smile. My dad would come home from work and would need to run an errand. "Deb, want to come along?" "Sure," I would say, and off we would go. He did not care what anyone thought – we would go skipping through the streets of New York City singing: Skip, Skip, Skip to my lou. On weekends when it would snow, he would pull my sister and me on the sled.

My mother worked on Saturdays. Many times dad, Evy and I would have an outing. The Saturdays he was home, trying to take his Shabbat nap. Nothing doing, dad! We would toss our socks on his face until he would get up. I would remind him that Mom never slept. Kids don't realize that working 18 hours some days could wear you out. He was never cross and would surrender to his girls when they wanted his attention.

It was devastating when my mother died ten days before I was leaving to go away to college. I offered to go to a local school or even to take a semester off. My dad did not want to hear anything of that. Education was highly valued in our family. I am grateful for my dad, who gave me the greatest gift: independence and the ability to support myself by providing for both my undergraduate and graduate degrees. He was always thrilled to hear about my continuing education, reminding me that whatever you learn no one can take away from you.

After my mother died when I was 19 years old, my dad had double duty. He had to see me through major medical issues from the time I was 20 years old. His optimism regarding the situation was helpful. He always helped me look at both sides of all options.

This book is for you, Dad. It is your story, one that you were finally able to share. You asked me to write down your experiences. I know it was a dark, painful, and a traumatic time. I know that reliving those memories robbed you of peaceful sleep. But now the task is done, and what you taught me, Dad, is that through the dark clouds the sun will eventually shine. Truly, despite your painful experiences, you are resilient. You embraced life. The sun is indeed shining. You and Mom had your personal victory over Hitler: two daughters and two grandchildren. Sadly, children were not to be for Danny and me. We shared our fur babies with you, always waiting for you to come up and sneak them a cookie or two. Danny joined me in my long search for family over the years. Time was always set aside during police memorial week to do research at the Holocaust Museum. Who would have known that many years later, with the help of the internet, my dream would come true. Family was found at long last. We have much to be grateful for. So here is to life and resilience! I thank you for everything you did for me throughout my life.

Love always, Deb, aka your favorite youngest daughter.

From Evy Lenoff, eldest daughter

"Any man can be a father but it takes someone special to be a dad." (Anne Geddes) A dad is someone who loves you unconditionally, is always there to support, give advice and protect. That sums up my dad, Hank Brodt. My Dad was a hard-working man who worked many hours, but took family responsibility very seriously and always wanted to have fun with his family.

Growing up, my mother used to tell me that she would hope that by the time my Dad came home from working overtime or a side job, I would be asleep so she would have peace and quiet. She knew that if I wasn't sleeping I would want a second dinner and it would be party time. What fun I had with my Dad playing and laughing. My

Mom worried that she would then have trouble getting me back to sleep, but my Dad would sing to me some of the many Jewish songs he knew and sleep would come.

Yearly, we would take a two-week vacation going to Ellenville, New York, staying at a bungalow company. It was there that I learned to square dance, twirling and laughing as my Dad spun me around. My Mom told me of another story from that vacation time. She was pushing me on the swing and I was having a wonderful time and a woman came up to me and said, "You must love your Mommy very much as you are having such fun." I was told that I responded, "Yes I love my Mommy, but I love my Daddy more!"

Saturdays, when I was a little older, Mom worked doing the books at a grocery store. That was when my sister Deb and I had our Dad to ourselves and what fun we had. He would try to take a Saturday afternoon nap and we bothered him so as we wanted him to play with us. Sometimes we won and he would play and other times we fell asleep with him.

Traditionally, Sunday was family day and we would leave our apartment and go to visit the many museums, go the Lower East Side, or to the many parks that New York had to offer. We would be permitted to get a hot pretzel or chestnuts from the street vendors as a treat. My favorite time of the year was the winter holidays. A carpenter by trade, Dad worked so very late and hard prior to Thanksgiving, helping with the beautiful decorations at Lord & Taylor. Mom would take us to see the glittering splendor and meet Dad for lunch. How proud he was of us as he introduced us to his co-workers. One year, for Chanukah, he found the time and surprised me with a beautiful handmade nightstand.

To this day, I remember it like it was yesterday. I was 10 years old and my Dad took me to see the new release Mary Poppins. I still see us skipping down the streets of our neighborhood singing Chim Chim Cheree. As I watch the movie today, tears fill my eyes at that *wonderful happy memory that I have of my Dad and me having that special time together.*

When I was finally old enough to drive, it was my Dad, with the patience of a saint, that took me practice driving and when I could afford it, helped me buy my first car, a 1969 blue Rambler, UGUxxx. I would drive my "new" car and whenever I heard a noise I would make him take it out and of course he heard nothing. Finally, after much frustration, he told me, "Turn the radio up and you won't hear a thing." I followed his advice until someone on the road said to me: "Lady, you are dragging your muffler." Dad then took the car out each time I heard a noise.

As I went away to college as a junior, so did my Mom. My Dad drove me to the University of Tennessee and I pleaded with him to allow me to keep my car with me, and he wouldn't as my Mom said no and we don't disobey Mom. He told me that he always supported the decisions my Mom made. He told me that one of the most important things he could do for his children was to love their mother and he truly loved, supported and believed in her. Once both Mom and I had a test at the same time. She did better on the test and Dad asked me why. I told him that I do the same chores as she does, such as laundry and preparing meals, but I also had to worry about what I would do Saturday night. He laughed and said he understood. My Dad was a softie. When it was my grandmother's 75th birthday and Mother's Day, I wanted to come home for the celebrations and Mom said you may not drive (I did finally get my car to college) and as I said earlier, you dared not disobey her. My Dad made sure I had an airline ticket to fly home to be part of the festivities and I really did surprise my Mom and of course her first question was: "How did you get here?" She wanted to be sure I didn't disobey and I simply answered that Dad sent me a ticket. One of the best things that my Dad did for me was to believe in me and to be sure that I had my college degree at no cost to me. I graduated not owing a dime. For that I will be eternally grateful.

Married 39 years, my wedding is a beautiful memory and I still hear him singing to me Sunrise, Sunset, *from* Fiddler on the Roof, *as we danced our father-daughter dance. When my children, his grandchildren, were born he was very excited to be an integral part of their lives, coming to Florida as often as he could to visit them. He is very proud of their accomplishments, as they are of his. My son Wayne has formed a special bond with him, accompanying him twice on the March of the Living and hearing his story. When my daughter Kaitlyn got married I asked him to do the Seven Blessings for the ceremony. He was not sure he could do it, but he stated when a daughter asks you to do something you do everything in your power to do it. It was a beautiful addition to the ceremony and he felt very important to be part of it.*

As my Dad approaches his 90th birthday, I am so blessed to have him as an important part of my life and treasure each day as I reflect on the many memories of day-to-day living and special holidays that we spent together.

Thank you for always being there to help and guide me through life and being my Dad. You are truly special to me.

With much love, Evy Lenoff, aka your favorite oldest daughter.

From Kaitlyn, granddaughter

I have a few memories I would like to share with you. As I was growing up you used to come visit me in Florida. We would swim and you taught me to play the game chimney sweep. We had such fun. As the years went by and I got older, I came up to New Jersey and visited you. You took me to dinner and to my first Broadway show: Beauty and the Beast. *We had such great seats, right in the center and not too far back. The most memorable and most recent* memory I have is when I called you on the phone to tell you I was getting married. You were so excited and couldn't wait for my special day. I asked you to do the Seven Blessings for my wedding and you did such a wonderful job. That will always be in my memory.

I love you!

Love you always and forever,

Your favorite granddaughter, Kaitlyn.

From Wayne, grandson

Living so far apart from you throughout my life has been a challenge. Life though is all about challenges, which is what I have learned from you. In the past five years, I have learned more from your experiences than one would hope to learn in a lifetime. The raw emotions of preparing for two separate March of the Living trips were a rollercoaster in themselves. I could have never imagined what it would be like to go to places that changed your life in so many ways and in turn changed mine. Listening to your experiences opened my eyes to enjoying life for what you have, to work hard and celebrate life.

I want to thank you for showing me where you came from and teaching me about the traditions that you celebrated as a child and adult. Those things are not only yours; they are where I came from too. Some things stand out clearly to me: earlier in life, coming up to New Jersey to experience a Giants game, the handshakes with the five dollars crumbled in your hand when we ended visits. Later in life through the March of the Living walking and dancing through the streets of Poland, getting off the plane in Israel feeling invigorated and alive, even though we were exhausted, walking through Israel when I was sick, looking for that magic liquor to make me feel better and learning that we *have an entire family in Israel that we now get to share on special occasions.*

Thank you for being MY grandfather, MY Pop Pop, I cherish the memories and lessons you have already given me, and I look forward to many more memories to come.

I Love You.

Wayne

From Bernie Slome, nephew

Today Hank Brodt is a man who shares his experiences as a Holocaust survivor. He travels and speaks wherever he is asked. He has been on the March of the Living numerous times. I am very proud of him.

To me, though, he is Uncle Henek. A man, a soldier, a friend and an uncle. I have had the pleasure of having him in my life for as long as I can remember. He was a young soldier, in his twenties, on leave about 1952, visiting us in Brooklyn. I never thought of him then as a survivor. After all, what survivor was in the army... and a sergeant no less, and I never heard him speak with an accent.

He was the man who led the second Seder night in his house where we, the family, gathered. He loved to sing. He made the Dayanu fun. He had this twinkle when he sang it. Sometimes a single chorus and sometimes a double chorus. Years later, after my dad passed away, the privilege of leading the Seder became mine. My uncle was there to help me and to lead the Dayanu. Although he no longer attends our Seders, my sons still do the Dayanu the way Uncle Hank did it. Sometimes the chorus is a single and sometimes a double; occasionally, just as he did, there was a third chorus.

Uncle Henek – I don't remember exactly when he became Uncle Hank – took me to Madison Square Garden to see Gene Autry. He took me to the circus and bought me cotton candy and a light on a lanyard that all the kids used to spin when the lights went down.

My first baseball game, Yankees vs. Detroit Tigers in 1958 at Yankee Stadium, was with my Uncle. My first Mets game, 1962 Polo Grounds against the Dodgers, was with my Uncle. We took the bus from his Washington Heights apartment and then walked a couple of blocks.

We played stickball at his Haverstraw bungalow colony. We played tennis at Shorehaven.

So many wonderful memories. So much laughter, so much fun. I am so lucky to have Uncle Hank in my life. He is a very special person.

Bernie Slome.

From Emil and the Israel Brodts

I remember well the event that happened in May, 2007. Oleg called me and gave a phone number in New Jersey. He said that he found that number on a website where the members of Jewish families could find one another. He said that this was the phone number of Mrs. Deborah Donnelly. Her father Herman Brodt was from Boryslaw, the town where my father, Simcha Brodt, was born.

I immediately called Deborah. When she heard who was calling she began to cry. "This is a miracle," she said. I tried to calm her down. I said that maybe it was just confusion. I asked to send pictures. And when I receive them I lost the last doubts. You, Hank, look so similar to my father!

And less than one month after this you came to Israel and we met. I'm happy that my mother could meet the brother of her late husband. It was a very exciting meeting. And all our next meetings in Israel and USA – all this is so nice.

Deb is right. It's a miracle that you, Hank, managed to keep alive during the Holocaust. A miracle that after so much time we could find one another and rejoin our family.

We all, Alex, Julia, Natasha, Oleg, Maxim, Ben, Yotam, and I, wish you continue to be as vigorous as we know you until now. Be healthy please, and be happy.

From Jason Weingarten, a family friend

It's one thing to talk about resilience in Holocaust survivors; it's another thing to witness it. As the grandson of two Holocaust survivors I had the privilege of being around those who demonstrated the very essence of what it means to be resilient in the face of prolonged trauma; it also meant that I was constantly thinking about the interplay of these two concepts: trauma and resilience. As a clinical psychologist I encounter the different trajectories that emerge from traumatic events and continue to be in awe of those who seem to make meaning – even grow – from such horrific experiences. So it was not surprising when I chose to focus my graduate studies on resilience in Holocaust survivors, astonished by their ability to persevere and finding the ways in which they reclaimed their agency worthy of not only admiration, but greater research and understanding.

As I read through the testimonies of Holocaust survivors, extracting and defining components and strategies embedded in their resilient journeys, certain themes and constructs emerged. It seems as though resilient Holocaust survivors embodied notions of hardiness, determination, and hope, reclaiming and restoring who they were while accepting, adapting and growing from the events that irreparably changed their lives. They lived with values of honor – honoring those who were lost, honoring their journey, and honoring their Jewish identity – and responsibility ("Never again"), often speaking of the better future that their children will have – while working endlessly to ensure it.

Hank Brodt is one of those people. Hank embraces the world with fierce determination, innate hope for a better future, and a hardy hug for those within arm's length. Since surviving the Holocaust, Hank has lived his life with the values of honor and responsibility as his guiding light. He has devoted so much of his time, effort, and heart into advocacy for Jewish causes and tributes to experiences he wishes no one has to endure again. I had the honor of spending many a Passover with Hank, captivated by his charisma and zest for life, endeared by his warmth and loving nature, and still in awe of what he did, what he does, and what he will continue to do, as I hope I get to spend another Passover with him soon, because people like Hank Brodt are few and far between.

From Rabbi Fred Guttman

Hank Brodt came to Greensboro a decade ago. I remember meeting him at services at our Greene Street Campus. He informed me that he was a Holocaust survivor who had been the unwelcome guest at five Nazi concentration camps.

As time went on, I asked Hank if he would consider going with us on the March of the Living. This annual odyssey to the concentration and death camps in Poland includes more than 10,000 teens from over 40 countries and concludes in Israel.

Hank was extremely reluctant at first. He really had no desire to go back to Poland and revisit the horror which he had not only experienced, but had been responsible for the death of almost all of his family.

I remember well the discussion in my office. I told him that if he chose to go with us, the trip would not be about him or about working out his feelings of loss and bereavement, no matter how difficult these feeling were. Rather, his participation on the trip would have a very different and holy mission, which would be to educate our young people about the tragedy of the Holocaust and how it had affected, in a terrible way, one Jew and his family. I also asked him how much longer he expected to live and how much longer he expected to be healthy enough to tell his story.

A week later, in 2006, Hank agreed to go on the trip with us. The impact of Hank's presence on the trip was immediate. Hank told his story often and in many places. He befriended our young people in a very special way. They, in essence, became his grandchildren and he became to them an additional zeyde. They even nicknamed him Hank the Tank!

I have seen youth listening to Hank with incredible intensity. I have seen them raise him on a chair like a Bar Mitzvah boy in a synagogue in Cracow. At the orphanage in Warsaw run by Janucz Korchak, I have heard Hank sing Oyfn Pripetshik, a song in memory of the 1,500,000 children who died. I have seen him dance with the kids on a disco boat on the Sea of Galilee. I have heard Hank sing the "veshamru" at a minyan of 200 or so males at the Kotel. I was present at the Hebrew Union College in Jerusalem on Shabbat in 2007, on the anniversary of Hank's liberation, when he was called for a special blessing.

In 2007 at Auschwitz (Birkenau), Hank was given the extraordinary honor of lighting one of the six memorial torches at the International Yom Hashoah (Holocaust) Memorial Day ceremony. He lit this torch in memory of the numerous members of his family who had been murdered by the Nazis.

While Hank was participating in the March of the Living, Hank's daughter Deborah received some welcome news. This news would change the ending of Hank's story and his life in a way that he could never imagine.

I could go on and on about my very dear friend Hank Brodt. He is truly a unique individual and the special experiences that we have shared are numerous.

Hank certainly did what I asked him to do and the result was that he went on not one March of the Living, but as of now, eight!

In our community, Hank continues to lecture at colleges, universities, high schools, middle schools and churches on the Shoah. In his words, he lectures to honor those who perished.

At the time of this writing Hank is approaching his ninetieth birthday. He has become an integral part of our Jewish community. He has a magnificent baritone voice and he frequently sings at Sabbath services at Temple Emanuel.

We wish him many more years of health, happiness and teaching young people about the horrible consequences of bias, bigotry, racism and antisemitism. Thank your Hank so very much for all that you have done to educate us, our children and the greater community!

Rabbi Fred Guttman.

ACKNOWLEDGMENTS

As the youngest daughter, I wrote down these memoirs by my father. In the process I received help from various people. I cannot thank my husband, Danny, enough for all of his help with this book and in everything that I do. Your patience and compassion during this process were invaluable. When I gave up totally overwhelmed by the pictures we saw, you persevered and discovered a picture of my dad the day after his liberation from Ebensee. For everything you do I cannot thank you enough. "I could curse the darkness or turn on a light." You are that light in all of the darkness throughout my life. I love you.

Evy, thank you for our highway discussions that led to the completion of this book. Decisions and agreements were forged as we were on our way to work.

To Howie Schechter, my mentor, my friend, thank you for encouraging me and reviewing my work. I appreciate your ability to help me focus and define my intended audience. Your support brought this book to fruition.

Dani of Organization of Boryslaw, Drohobycz and vicinity, thank you so much for the pictures and history of the Galicia region. My dad always tells me that "Galicianos" are the nicest people. I see that for myself.

To Nancy Hartman and colleagues from the United States Holocaust Memorial Museum, I cannot thank you enough for your help with obtaining the pictures for this book. Nancy, thank you for giving me a picture of my father when he was 19 years old. Sadly this is the only picture of him that we have from his youth.

Early into this project my father introduced me to Chris Cox who initially wanted to write my father's memoirs but was told I was doing just that. I now have to thank Chris who offered his expertise serving as a writing consultant to the earlier drafts. Not only did I enjoy Chris's thick sudden drawl but his encouragement and kindness. Thank you Chris for all of your support.

Wayne and Kaitlyn, thank you for being the most wonderful niece and nephew one can have. I appreciate your feedback and for volunteering to write something to your grandfather. Thank you Stuart for being my brother-in-law, your honesty is always appreciated and gave me many laughs.

Bernie and Roz, you cannot choose your family but you can choose who you would like to spend time with. Thank you for being there at critical times as it relates to my dad's story. You were by my side as we were discovering that we had actually found my cousins. Your keen eyes were very instrumental in pursuing this miracle. Thank you for participating in this book, bringing out that my dad is so much more than a survivor. Thank you for writing a letter to him to be included.

My dear Tori, thank you for bringing my vision for the cover of the book to life. You are a talented photographer and a wonderful human being. I am blessed to have such a great adopted daughter.

To Oleg, thank you for looking on Jewish Gen FamilyFinder.

Thank you to Oleg, Max, Emil, Alex, Natasha, Julia and Guidon for helping me know a part of our family history and helping make up for too much lost time. Due to my dad's young age when his dad died, we had little information about his father. Together I think we have as complete a family history as possible.

To all my friends and colleagues, thank you for everything that you did to support my efforts in writing this book. Many of you were that ray of sunshine I needed as I researched this very dark period in time. I am truly blessed to have such wonderful friends.

To my kindred spirit Liesbeth Heenk of Amsterdam Publishers, thank you for taking a chance on me and my father's memoirs. You challenged me to keep going as you continued to raise the bar. You are an awesome publisher. Thank you for renewing my faith.

To my dad, I cannot say it enough, how sorry I am for all that you endured at such a young age. You are truly the epitome of resilience. Your optimism and faith in others are just some of your wonderful qualities. I am lucky to have you as my dad. Being a survivor is just a small part of who you are to Evy and me. You are our dad, the one we ran to when we were scared, the one who taught us to drive, the one who listened to our tales of woe and always the one who pushed us forward. I stand with you in saying Never Forget and Never Again.

EPILOGUE

Hank Brodt sadly passed away on May 22, 2020

What do you say about a loved one after they die that has more meaning than the Obituary and the Eulogies spoken. It is always painful beyond belief in those days, weeks and months that follow. My dad died during the Covid-19 pandemic – his death getting lost in the numbers but not for me. For me, he is not a statistic! Did he die from Covid-19 people queried? No, is the response, not technically. What is the difference anyway, death is death. However, back to Covid-19, there was no malice intended in the demise of my father. To put it simply, the health care system across our great nation was on overload. There was also a war waging between my dad's innate programming to survive and his body that was in the process of giving out. He lost his mobility in his final days due to hospitalization. His mobility was his survival, his independence. My dad always stated: "I want to be my own man." He fought my sister Evy and myself in coming to live near one of us. He repeatedly stated that he did not want to be a burden, most of all he wanted to "make his own way." Evy and I told him quite bluntly, that as long as he lived so far away, he was putting stress on both of us. What our dad robbed us of are the actions of love for our father that are more important than words. Showing him love, care and dignity in those final days were choices we were trying to make. We wanted to show him the love of daughters for their father.

When we saw my father's strength waning, my husband Danny and I immediately drove down to North Carolina. We were there for only a few days when the facility no longer allowed visitors as the pandemic was raging. They were limiting outsiders from entering their buildings to prevent the spread of infections. There was no use in remaining in North Carolina. I could best follow my father's care from the comfort of my home. So we left and headed north only to find all the rest stops along the corridor closed due the pandemic.

When my father fell ill a few weeks later, hospitals were not permitting visitors. Despite my pleas they had a no-visitor policy to limit the spread of the Corona virus. When my dad returned to the facility we again could not visit. When he went on hospice I was eager to see him, but neither my rheumatologist nor primary doctor would allow me to fly – let alone drive – and find a place to stop somewhere. As my dad had both a landline and cell phone I kept in contact more often than not. My dad was able to respond to me until the final 24 hours of his life. As his caregivers held the phone to his ear I would talk and sing to him. Of course being driven by emotion I would also sob uncontrollably. In response he would say in Polish: "I love you, please don't cry."

Evy finally made it from Florida to the facility to be with him as our survivor surrendered to his body. My father left this world in every sense being his own man.

His funeral plans were made by himself, close to when my mother died. What we did not count on were all the Executive Orders that varied from state to state during the Pandemic. In New Jersey we were not permitted to have large gatherings including burials.

Funeral services as we knew it pre-Covid did not exist. Hence, my father's funeral was just a burial with five of us in attendance, consisting of immediate family and one close friend. There were no other rituals that we came to depend on as part of the grief journey.

I started grieving well in advance of his demise and continued long after. If I continued on my path of crying and grieving, my parents would have been furious not to mention disappointed. "Life is for the living," both of them would say. "We want you to live and embrace life. After all both of you are our personal victories over Hitler." It has been almost seven months, I am still sad and have my moments that I am entitled to. When we love, we risk great sadness that accompanies loss.

While my dad was a Holocaust Survivor my husband Danny described my dad best as a man always being "at the ready." Tools in hand, he would appear at our house to offer assistance.

As I now reflect back on happier days, I recall how he would come up to play with our dogs and give them a treat or two. When travelling became challenging, we brought the dogs, driving over 600 miles to visit. He was in his glory, so happy to see them. No matter where in the house my dad would go, he would have his canine entourage. If he took a nap, the grand dogs were snoozing right there with him. With a smile on my face I can see my dad and saying in his thick Polish accent "Hello dowggies" [Hello Doggies].

As the sun was setting on his life, he realized the importance of sharing his experiences during the Holocaust. Many survivors were dying off that were old enough to have witnessed and understand what had happened. He was the last man standing in his social group from Poland.

Now my dad's family and countless others have a responsibility to go forth and retell his story, as he and other survivors are rapidly becoming a part of history.

Before his demise, my dad put down his hammer and became a teacher. His lesson was what happens when hate and blame get out of control. This horror cannot die with him and others. As 2 and 3Gs we especially have a responsibility. You as readers have now agreed to share this responsibility, to stand up to Holocaust deniers. It happened. Hate sadly continues into the present.

As we are linked generation to generation please be kind and accepting of our differences. Honor my dad's memory and tell his and other survivors' stories. Speak of the six million Jews and millions of others who died for the mere crime of being different. Speak of our American heroes, our military that died trying to stop a mad man's ideology. Speak of how in the 1940s a country saluted for being the birthplace of culture tried to exterminate the Jewish population of Europe.

My dad wanted to be his own man. And that is what he did. Some might gasp at what I am about to say. One day my dad looked at me and said: "Debs, how long are we suppose to go and carry this hate. I think it is time to forgive." With conviction in his voice, my dad stated "It is time to forgive but – make no mistake – I will never forget!!"

When you think of my dad, I hope it is with a smile on your face. He was more than just a survivor. He was a carpenter and educator. He was my dad. The man who could be counted on at the spur of a moment. The man who was his own man and knew about resilience. He asked very little of us. "Never Forget."

For my dad

He was getting old, and he knew the world must be told. Lies you say IT NEVER HAPPENED. No one can be so cruel.

He was getting old and the truth that he witnessed was buried so deep in his soul. It had to emerge and the world had to be told.

Six million died solely for their worship to G-d and millions others because it was said that they were simply subpar.

Many came to stand and fight against the cruelty and insanity. They lost their lives standing by the meaning of Old Glory.

He was getting old and knew his story must be told. Lest we forget that all are here on this earth perfect in our maker's soul.

He was getting old and knew what he had lived through must be told. So he reached down into his very core and the story was finally told.

He raised his children to look beyond one's appearance and race. Instead, he said look within their hearts and soul.

The sun has set and his story has been told. It's now up to you to set his story free.

–Deborah Donnelly, December 2020 (Epilogue), and June 2020 (Poem)

Memorial Kathe Brodt

Memorial Hank Brodt

PICTURES

Hank in 1948

Hank, the proud American Soldier (1951)

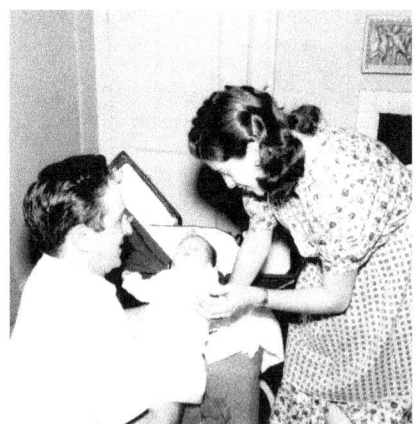

Hank and Kathe fuss over their new born baby girl,
Evy (1954)

The Brodt family: Deborah, Hank, Evy and Kathe
(1961)

Hank and Kathe dance at the wedding of Evy and
Stuart (August 1976)

Hank and Kathe smiling despite difficult times
(November 1977)

Hank with his daughters Evy and Deborah as they
get ready to leave the house for Deborah's wedding
(July 1988)

Wedding of Deborah and Dan (July 1988) Standing
left-right: Bruce Slome (Holocaust Survivor), Bernie
Slome, Hank, Wayne, Deborah, Dan, Evy & Stuart.
Sitting left-right: Ruth Slome, Kaitlyn and Rozzi
Slome

Hank with family and hometown friend Abe
(Holocaust Survivor), standing second from left. Also
present are Rozzi's parents Norbert and Sophie
Kugel (both Holocaust survivors)

Hank with his nephew Emil and his wife Julia in Israel
(2007)

Hank with granddaughter Kaitlyn at her wedding
(June 2012)

Evy, Hank & Deborah at Kaitlyn's wedding (June 2012)

Rabbi Fred Guttman and Hank during the March of the Living 2014, sharing a quiet moment at the Warsaw Cemetery.

Hank and Oleg in deep conversation during visit to Israel (2014)

Hank visiting his newly found family members in
Israel (2014)

Hank's 90th birthday with Alex from Israel and
daughter Deborah (December 2015)

Hank with his grandchildren and spouses at Wayne
and Miriam's wedding (March 2016)

Hank Brodt and his daughter Deborah holding his
memoirs (January 2017)

Hank Brodt leading singing Hatikvah, Israeli National
anthem at Krakow Philharmonic in April 2018 (behind
him is Israel's Ambassador to the US Ron Dermer),
Photo by Ivan Cutler © Courtesy of the International
March of the Living.

Hank Brodt leading singing Hatikvah, Israeli National anthem at Krakow Philharmonic in April 2018, Photo by Ivan Cutler © Courtesy of the International March of the Living.

Hank Brodt sadly passed away on 22 May 2020. Sketch for his memorial, designed by Koch monument, Hackensack, NJ.

NOTES

1. According to the *Encyclopedia Judaica Virtual Jewish History*, Boryslaw, now part of the Ukraine, is a city rich in history. At the end of the 19th century, it was nicknamed the 'California of Galicia'. During the Roaring Twenties, Boryslaw provided 75 per cent of the oil used in Poland. Much of the oil industry was built around the hard work of Jewish people.

The neighboring town of Drohobycz was home to the oil refineries. As many as 3,000 Jewish people from Boryslaw and neighboring communities earned their living by holding various jobs in the oil industry. As this industry became modernized, larger corporations with access to more money forced out Jewish labor, although some of the wells were still owned by Jewish people. As a result the Jewish people had a sense of belonging for this area of Galicia. They earned a living, and had places of worship. Additionally, the Jewish communities of Boryslaw and Drohobycz joined together and established a cultural and religious center.

Their socio-economic status varied from family to family. While the Jewish population fluctuated during the oil boom, in 1939 there were over 13,000 Jewish people living in Boryslaw. Some research (*Jewish Virtual*) shows the Jewish population just prior to World War II as being around 15,000 people. According to the Organization of Drohobycz, Boryslaw and its vicinity, the region had approximately 200 Jewish survivors after World War II. Entire families were eliminated, and this was only one fragment of the atrocity that was unfolding all across Europe as the Nazis systematically murdered six million Jews. The Holocaust will always be regarded as one of human history's darkest chapters. One of my frequently asked questions concerns the magnitude and implications of the millions murdered by Hitler and his regime: What if the cure for cancer, lupus, diabetes and other diseases might have been discovered by one of the victims? This is just one of the endless number of maddening questions for which we will never have an answer.

2. Sources consulted for this publication:

Jewish Virtual Library, www.jewishvirtuallibrary.org, a project of the American-Israeli Cooperative Enterprise, consulted February 8, 2016

Yad Vashem. The World Holocaust Remembrance Center, www. yadvashem.org consulted March 18, 2016

Jewish GenFamily Finder on Boryslaw Drohobycz Administration District www.JewishGen.org\jgff, consulted February 2015-July 2016

Organization of Drohobycz, Boryslaw and the vicinity for survivors and their descendants, www.drohobycz-boryslaw.org\organization consulted July 16, 2016

United States Holocaust Memorial Museum, www.ushmm.org

Brief History of the Jews of Drohobycz and Boryslaw compiled by William Fern for the Drohobycz-Boryslaw reunion, held May 3-5, 1985 at the Pines Hotel in South Fallsburg, NY Holocaust

Research Project – Holocaust Education and Archive Research Team – Plaszow, Mauthausen Concentration Camps www. holocaustresearchproject.org

Steven Spielberg Shoah Project, Hank Brodt interview DVD, owned by author

USC Shoah Foundation sfi.usc.edu

World War II award-winning documentary by Frank Capra distributed by Madacy Entertainment Group, 1997

3. This was a unique skill. The practice may sound grotesque to modern readers who are fortunate to live in the age of modern medicine where antibiotics are available to cure a variety of illnesses. In those days, leeches were placed on the body to feed on blood. Along with the blood, out came the bacteria or poisons causing the illness. Mechanical leeching worked in a similar way. Live leeches were not used. Instead the mechanical leech brought the harmful poisons to the surface of the skin, clearing the body of the culprits causing the illness. Mechanical leeching is still used today in some places and circumstances.

4. His title was *Judensachbearbeiter bei der Dienststelle des SS- und Polizeiführers Galizien in Lemberg und Inspekteur des jüdischen ZAL im Distrikt Galizien.*

5. Whenever I speak and talk about Plaszow, I am always asked if I was on Schindler's list. The truth is that I knew nothing of Schindler or his list. There were many factories near Krakow, but I was not from the area. I salute Oscar Schindler for what he did to help many survive. If there would have been more people like Oscar Schindler, more would have survived the Nazi death machine.

6. At the trial of the Supreme National Tribunal of Poland, Krakow, from August 27-31 and September 2-5, 1946, Amon Goeth was found guilty and hanged.

7. The famous picture with emaciated prisoners taken on the day of the liberation of their camp is actually a photo taken at Ebensee on May 6, 1945.

KIND REQUEST

If you have enjoyed reading my father's memoirs,
please do leave a review on Amazon or Goodreads. A few kind
words would be enough. This would be greatly appreciated.

Alternatively, if you have read this as Kindle eBook, you could
simply leave a rating.
That is just one click, indicating how many stars of five you think
this book deserves.
This will only cost you a split second.
Thank you very much in advance!

Deborah Donnelly

For enquiries about lectures, please get in touch with the author
Acandleandapromise@gmail.com

For all other enquiries (books or author's manuscripts) please get in
touch with the publisher:
info@amsterdampublishers.com

AMSTERDAM PUBLISHERS
HOLOCAUST LIBRARY

The series **Holocaust Survivor Memoirs World War II** consists of the following autobiographies of survivors:

Outcry. Holocaust Memoirs, by Manny Steinberg

Hank Brodt Holocaust Memoirs. A Candle and a Promise, by Deborah Donnelly

The Dead Years. Holocaust Memoirs, by Joseph Schupack

Rescued from the Ashes. The Diary of Leokadia Schmidt, Survivor of the Warsaw Ghetto, by Leokadia Schmidt

My Lvov. Holocaust Memoir of a twelve-year-old Girl, by Janina Hescheles

Remembering Ravensbrück. From Holocaust to Healing, by Natalie Hess

Wolf. A Story of Hate, by Zeev Scheinwald with Ella Scheinwald

Save my Children. An Astonishing Tale of Survival and its Unlikely Hero, by Leon Kleiner with Edwin Stepp

Holocaust Memoirs of a Bergen-Belsen Survivor & Classmate of Anne Frank, by Nanette Blitz Konig

Defiant German - Defiant Jew. A Holocaust Memoir from inside the Third Reich, by Walter Leopold with Les Leopold

In a Land of Forest and Darkness. The Holocaust Story of two Jewish Partisans, by Sara Lustigman Omelinski

Holocaust Memories. Annihilation and Survival in Slovakia, by Paul Davidovits

From Auschwitz with Love. The Inspiring Memoir of Two Sisters' Survival, Devotion and Triumph Told by Manci Grunberger Beran & Ruth Grunberger Mermelstein, by Daniel Seymour

Remetz. Resistance Fighter and Survivor of the Warsaw Ghetto, by Jan Yohay Remetz

My March Through Hell. A Young Girl's Terrifying Journey to Survival, by Halina Kleiner with Edwin Stepp

Roman's Journey, by Roman Halter

Beyond Borders. Escaping the Holocaust and Fighting the Nazis. 1938-1948, by Rudi Haymann

The Engineers. A memoir of survival through World War II in Poland and Hungary, by Henry Reiss

Memoirs by Elmar Rivosh, Sculptor (1906-1967). Riga Ghetto and Beyond, by Elmar Rivosh

Defying Death on the Danube. A Holocaust Survival Story, by Debbie J. Callahan with Henry Stern

A Doorway to Heroism. A decorated German-Jewish Soldier who became an American Hero, by Rabbi W. Jack Romberg

The Shoemaker's Son. The Life of a Holocaust Resister, by Laura Beth Bakst

The Redhead of Auschwitz. A True Story, by Nechama Birnbaum

Land of Many Bridges. My Father's Story, by Bela Ruth Samuel Tenenholtz

Creating Beauty from the Abyss. The Amazing Story of Sam Herciger, Auschwitz Survivor and Artist, by Lesley Ann Richardson

On Sunny Days We Sang. A Holocaust Story of Survival and Resilience, by Jeannette Grunhaus de Gelman

Painful Joy. A Holocaust Family Memoir, by Max J. Friedman

I Give You My Heart. A True Story of Courage and Survival, by Wendy Holden

In the Time of Madmen, by Mark A. Prelas

Monsters and Miracles. Horror, Heroes and the Holocaust, by Ira Wesley Kitmacher

Flower of Vlora. Growing up Jewish in Communist Albania, by Anna Kohen

Aftermath: Coming of Age on Three Continents. A Memoir, by Annette Libeskind Berkovits

Not a real Enemy. The True Story of a Hungarian Jewish Man's Fight for Freedom, by Robert Wolf

Zaidy's War. Four Armies, Three Continents, Two Brothers. One Man's Impossible Story of Endurance, by Martin Bodek

The Glassmaker's Son. Looking for the World my Father left behind in Nazi Germany, by Peter Kupfer

The Apprentice of Buchenwald. The True Story of the Teenage Boy Who Sabotaged Hitler's War Machine, by Oren Schneider

Good for a Single Journey, by Helen Joyce

Burying the Ghosts. She escaped Nazi Germany only to have her life torn apart by the woman she saved from the camps: her mother, by Sonia Case

American Wolf. From Nazi Refugee to American Spy. A True Story, by Audrey Birnbaum

Bipolar Refugee. A Saga of Survival and Resilience, by Peter Wiesner

Before the Beginning and After the End, by Hymie Anisman

Malka Owsiany recounts, by Mark Turkow (editor)

I Will Give Them an Everlasting Name. Jacksonville's Stories of the Holocaust, by Samuel P. Cox

The series **Jewish Children in the Holocaust** consists of the
following autobiographies of Jewish children
hidden during WWII in the Netherlands:

Searching for Home. The Impact of WWII on a Hidden Child, by
Joseph Gosler

See You Tonight and Promise to be a Good Boy! War memories, by
Salo Muller

Sounds from Silence. Reflections of a Child Holocaust Survivor,
Psychiatrist and Teacher, by Robert Krell

Sabine's Odyssey. A Hidden Child and her Dutch Rescuers, by
Agnes Schipper

The Journey of a Hidden Child, by Harry Pila and Robin Black

The series **New Jewish Fiction** consists of the following novels, written by Jewish authors. All novels are set in the time during or after the Holocaust.

The Corset Maker. A Novel, by Annette Libeskind Berkovits

Escaping the Whale. The Holocaust is over. But is it ever over for the next generation? by Ruth Rotkowitz

When the Music Stopped. Willy Rosen's Holocaust, by Casey Hayes

Hands of Gold. One Man's Quest to Find the Silver Lining in Misfortune, by Roni Robbins

The Girl Who Counted Numbers. A Novel, by Roslyn Bernstein

There was a garden in Nuremberg. A Novel, by Navina Michal Clemerson

The Butterfly and the Axe, by Omer Bartov

To Live Another Day. A Novel, Elizabeth Rosenberg

A Worthy Life. Based on a True Story, by Dahlia Moore

The series **Holocaust Heritage** consists of the following memoirs by 2G:

The Cello Still Sings. A Generational Story of the Holocaust and of the Transformative Power of Music, by Janet Horvath

The Fire and the Bonfire. A Journey into Memory, by Ardyn Halter

The Silk Factory: Finding Threads of My Family's True Holocaust Story, by Michael Hickins

Hidden in Plain Sight. A Journey into Memory and Place, by Julie Brill

Winter Light: The Memoir of a Child of Holocaust Survivors, by Grace Feuerverger

The series **Holocaust Books for Young Adults** consists of the following novels, based on true stories:

The Boy behind the Door. How Salomon Kool Escaped the Nazis. Inspired by a True Story, by David Tabatsky

Running for Shelter. A True Story, by Suzette Sheft

The Precious Few. An Inspirational Saga of Courage based on True Stories, by David Twain with Art Twain

The series **WWII Historical Fiction** consists of the following novels, some of which are based on true stories:

Mendelevski's Box. A Heartwarming and Heartbreaking Jewish Survivor's Story, by Roger Swindells

A Quiet Genocide. The Untold Holocaust of Disabled Children in WWII Germany, by Glenn Bryant

The Knife-Edge Path, by Patrick T. Leahy

Brave Face. The Inspiring WWII Memoir of a Dutch/German Child, by I. Caroline Crocker and Meta A. Evenbly

When We Had Wings. The Gripping Story of an Orphan in Janusz Korczak's Orphanage. A Historical Novel, by Tami Shem-Tov

Jacob's Courage. Romance and Survival amidst the Horrors of War, by Charles S. Weinblatt

Join the AP Review Team

Reviews are very important in a world dominated by the social media. Feedback for Holocaust books is more than just a customer review; it also shows the relevance and importance of such books in today's society.

Please go over to the AmsterdamPublishers.com website (top of page) if you want to join the *AP review team,* showing **at least one review on Amazon** for one of our books. You will get updates about new releases and will get the chance to read and review.